Evidence is Lacking. Yet I Still Hope.

A Primary Source Glimpse into a World War I Soldier's Life... Home to Camp Lewis to France

by Joan Enders

Alpine Books
Longview, WA

Alpine Books
25 Alpine Way
Longview, Washington 98632

The text font is Garamond.
Book design by Joan Enders.

Discounted classroom sets are available in sets of 10 , 20 or 30 books.
Custom color primary source material sets, teacher webinars, on-site teacher training, and student debriefings via webinar are available.
See the author 's website at JoanEnders.com for more information.

Library of Congress Cataloging-in-Publication Data
Enders, Joan.
"Evidence is Lacking. Yet I Still Hope" : A Primary Source Glimpse into a World War I Soldier's Life...
Home to Camp Lewis to France /
by Joan Enders.
p. cm.
Includes bibliographical references.
978-0-9990144-0-0
World War, 1914-1918--Biography. 2. World War, 1914-1918--Interactive book. 3. Soldiers--United States--Biography. 4. Bates, Joshua Henry--Journals. 5. World War, 1914-1918--France. 6. World War, 1914-1918--Meuse-Argonne Campaign. 7. World War, 1914-1918--Camp Lewis (Fort Lewis)—Personal narratives. 8. World War, 1914-1918--91st Division, 347th Machine Gun Battalion. 9. World War, 1914-1918--Primary Sources. 10. Primary Sources--World War, 1914-1918.

2017
940.4
Library of Congress Control Number: 2017942663

~To my colleague at the Robert A. Long High School History Department, JD Ott, who trusted my idea.

~To Uncle Josh.

Evidence is Lacking. Yet I Still Hope.

A Primary Source Glimpse into a World War I Soldier's Life... Home to Camp Lewis to France

Preface

My cousin entered, hefting a box of letters, photographs, certificates and *realia* belonging to our uncle, Joshua Henry Bates. Coupled with records saved by my mother, we had a document scanning frenzy of genealogical-nirvana proportions. As other cousins discovered our fun, a journal materialized. A secretary desk Joshua built was unveiled. Missing portraits reappeared.

As a high school librarian I wished that *my* students could be as excited about history as we were. With one crass, nepotistic decision, I developed a learning experience in which our U.S. History students would learn about Joshua Henry Bates by digging deeper into the concise, genuine, American primary sources that my family had preserved.

Joshua was a young adult. He had a girl friend. He loved dancing. He was a soldier. There was enough fodder to pique student curiosity. Was there enough to pique instructor interest?

I introduced the inquiry-learning experience in a social studies grant workshop. Teachers dug deep into the primary sources to find and analyze information about the young adult life of Joshua Henry Bates. They were to research as if they were to produce a scholarly narrative of his life. One teacher was so enthused that he began researching his own family history. Another, JD Ott, responded in the way I hoped: "Joan, what are the chances of my APUSH (Advanced Placement U.S. History) students having this same lesson?" Our first lesson started on November 11, Armistice Day. As we facilitated (educational nirvana) the inquiry, student comments wafted up from the tables:

"Poor Rena!"
"This makes me cry!"
"One source says October 3rd, and others say October 4th."
"His writing is messy."
"This is so stupid." (day one)
"No, here's the answer." (day two, same student)
"Why does this telegram have a September date?"
"What's in that window?"
"There's too many Joshuas."

Students learned to extrapolate by focusing on minutia and collecting facts that the sources divulged. Each year at least one student excavated information that I overlooked. That always amazed me.

Teams strategically divided and conquered the materials. No lectures were needed. Not that some students did not stonewall. But the intrigue of the quest won out after only one rotation to the next set of clues. I was confident that students would immerse themselves in this inquiry learning experience. Nonetheless I did not anticipate the level of attachment they would form with Josh. Each year at least one student shed tears. One informed me that she wanted everything I had in my possession about Joshua in order to write a book about him.

Young adults do enjoy discovery through inquiry. Furthermore, they *are* interested in a personal history, a history to which they can relate. My students viscerally "adopted" Joshua. It went further. Students wanted to know who *they* were and who their ancestors were. Students asked relatives if family members served in World War I.

The effect of such family stories has been studied and documented by Marshall P. Duke and Robyn Fivush of Emory University who concluded that "teenagers who know their family histories are more likely to show higher levels of social and emotional health." They recorded family dinner conversations to learn more about how families shared their stories. " 'One of the big tasks of adolescence is [deciding] who you want to be in the world: occupation, religion, values, what kind of person do you want to be,' said psychologist Robyn Fivush, who co-authored the study of 2009. 'Family stories offer lessons that help teens shape their identities,' she said. The researchers said that it is likely that the knowledge itself does not cause these benefits, but the fact that it reflects a cohesive family structure and systems that benefit the teens (Chandler)."

After six years of primary sources research and scholarly narrative writing about Joshua H. Bates' tour of duty, students had an appreciation for and connection with the sacrifices of the AEF in the forests of France as conveyed through the story of one young soldier. Teachers and I assessed the experience and tweaked the plan, forms, delivery, assignment and assessment; but the powerful inquiry experience remained.

Since that first year in 2008, we presented our case study at the National Social Studies Conference 2012, then at the Washington Library Media Association Conference in 2013. In 2014 I went solo, facilitating youth at the Brigham Young University *Genealogy and Family History Conference*, followed by a how-to session for adults. In 2015 we presented at the Lower Columbia Genealogical Society and community groups. Though the original inquiry experience was created for high school students, I discovered that adults became as invested in the experience as the youth. Since that time the creation of this interactive book and its editing into a useable tool has been my focus.

My hope is that readers can replicate the enjoyment, curiosity and critical observation as they scour primary and secondary sources about Joshua H. Bates, a Camp Lewis soldier, a soldier of the American Expeditionary Forces in France. This book contains far more material than we used in our inquiry lessons. When used for instruction, some of the material will need to be sifted and gleaned for the inquiry experience. This book is intended for individual use and as reference, not a workbook for a classroom. That would defeat the inquiry experience.

Joan Enders

Introduction

Read this!
No, no, no! Don't turn the page!
Really, this is where you need to start.

The purpose of this book is to introduce you to a variety of primary sources that you may encounter in research or in family history or American primary documents, and to arm you with the ability to squeeze out information about a specific person from the document.

Let's keep it real. Does a history detective read history textbooks, fill out worksheets and watch historical movies? Nope! Sam Wineberg, a master at detection of clues, says:

> *"...when you ask historians what they do, a different picture emerges. They see themselves as detectives searching for evidence among primary sources to a mystery that can never be completely solved. Wouldn't this image be more enticing to a bored high school student?"* [1]

Start an investigation with me. Let's uncover clues about a person's life, gumshoeing through the documents. Can we reconstruct a life through our detective work?

Family historians' advise to start a search with the saved "stuff" in a shoebox under the stairs or closet or garage. Those records are what I am talking about when I mention primary sources: newspaper clippings, certificates, school awards, report cards, letters, photographs, journals, mementos, dried corsages...you get the idea.

Keep in mind that the original documents are around 100 years old. Some are worn or damaged or faded. Others are in wonderful shape. Some are originally in color, but changed to black and white for the book. I mention this as the items, even pages in a journal, vary in quality.

Each chapter will introduce one or more sources for investigation and dissection. The items will divulge information about the person who is the subject of this book. These questions will help:

Who created the item?
What makes the item unique?
What it the title?
What is its date?
Who/what is the item about?
What suspect clues are discovered?
What makes it an excellent item?
What makes it a poor item?
What does it tell me about my suspect?

You can either scribble in this book, or use paper for notes. Just do not photocopy the book. Every item is about one, real person. Your mission is to find out so much about the suspect that you *could* write a narrative about the person.

Scattered between the chapters are a few pages called "Insights" that give more information about a chapter. I share my analysis of the primary sources toward the end of the book in a section called "My Findings." Resist peeking until you have finished each chapter. *I predict that you will be an excellent detective.*

A victim? A villain? A hero? What will your investigation reveal?

Chapter 1: The Suspect

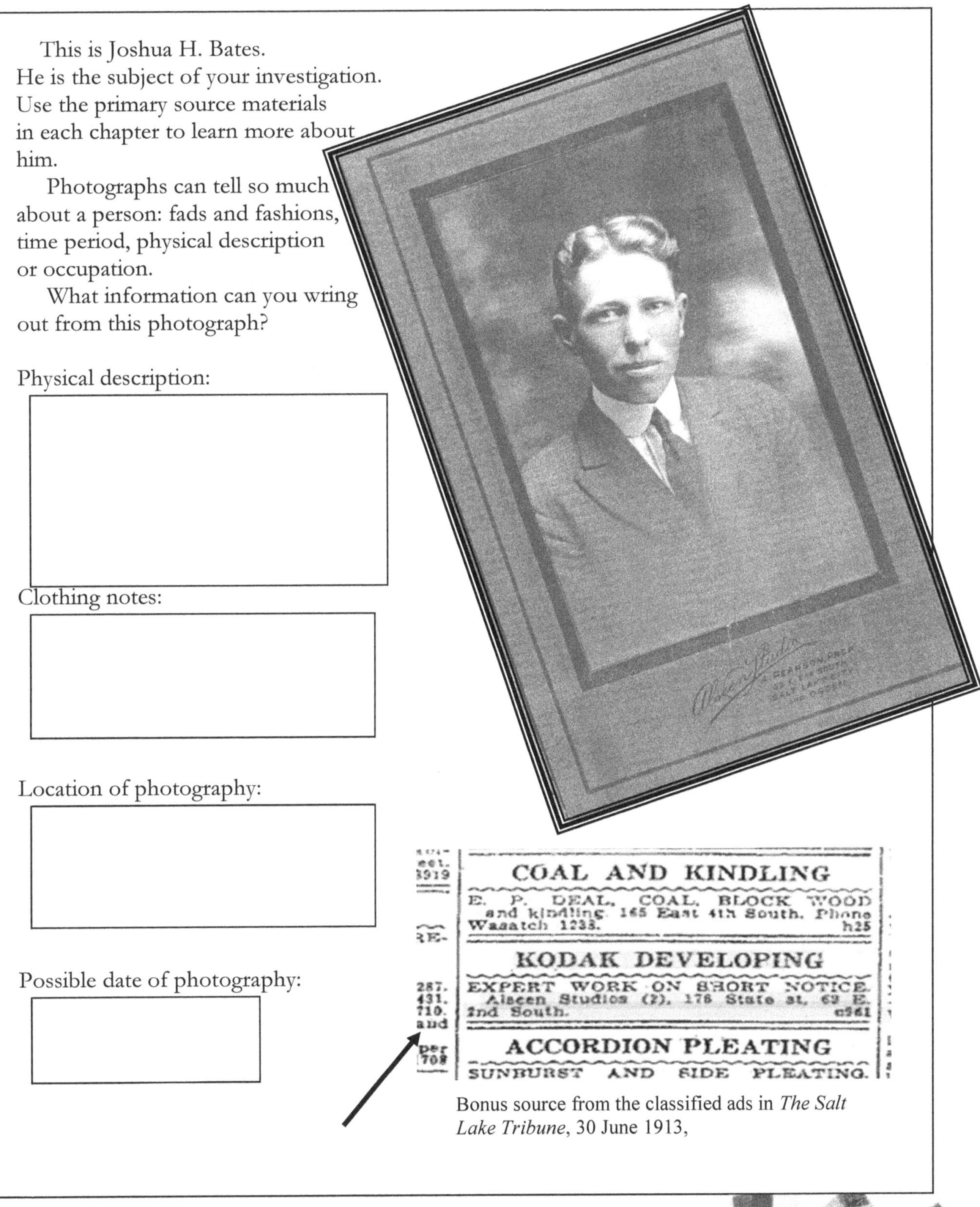

This is Joshua H. Bates. He is the subject of your investigation. Use the primary source materials in each chapter to learn more about him.

Photographs can tell so much about a person: fads and fashions, time period, physical description or occupation.

What information can you wring out from this photograph?

Physical description:

Clothing notes:

Location of photography:

Possible date of photography:

COAL AND KINDLING

E. P. DEAL, COAL, BLOCK WOOD and kindling. 165 East 4th South. Phone Wasatch 1233. h25

KODAK DEVELOPING

EXPERT WORK ON SHORT NOTICE. Alseen Studios (2), 176 State st, 69 E. 2nd South. c961

ACCORDION PLEATING

SUNBURST AND SIDE PLEATING.

Bonus source from the classified ads in *The Salt Lake Tribune*, 30 June 1913,

Chapter 2: Starting at the End

Obituaries, or short biographical sketches of a deceased person, are an amazing source of information. Though a secondary source, an obituary can contain many clues to a person's life.

Here is Joshua H. Bates' obituary. Your mission is to list every scrap of information about him that you find in it.

Summit County Boy Dies For World Liberty

(Special Correspondence.)

WANSHIP, Summit Co., Nov. 20.—Mr. and Mrs. Joshua Bates have a telegram from the war department announcing the death of their son, Private Joshua H. Bates.

JOSHUA H. BATES.

Private Bates went to Camp Lewis in September, 1917, where he received his training. He was a member of the 347th machine gun battalion. He landed in France July 23, 1918. The telegram stated he was killed Oct. 4, while operating his machine gun.

Private Bates was a native of Wanship and was 23 years of age. He was a graduate of the North Summit high school. He studied two summers at the University of Utah and for two years was principal of the Wanship school. He leaves a father, mother, three brothers and two sisters.

1.

2.

3.

4.

5.

6.

7.

8.

9.

10.

11.

12.

What important information did it add that you could not discern from a photograph alone?

Why is a newspaper obituary a secondary or even a tertiary source? Explain your answer.

Insights: The Census of The United States

Family Search International has an excellent article on the United States census in its "Beginning United States Research" wiki article. Use it for detailed information and internal links about the census. But for now, here are some basics about the United States census to help you understand why Joshua Henry Bates' information for 1900 and 1910 is recorded.

The census is an inventory of people who live in the United States, taken every ten years. The numbers of people in each state, county and town are used to determine the representation of the citizens of the United States in the House of Representatives of the United States Congress. Censuses are also know as "population schedules." The enumerator, or census taker, writes down individual "'snapshots" of people in each household with specific questions, on the particular day of his or her visit. People are required to answer truthfully but some are creative with ages, names and nicknames.

The first federal census was in 1790. States were included in a census once they achieved statehood, and there were some territorial censuses. Anyone can read any census that is 72 years old, up to and including the 1940 census. In 2022 the 1950 census will be released to the public. There will be a flurry of indexers recording the information in it so that persons in that census can be found in online genealogical databases.

Not all censuses are created equally. Some have clues into a person's heritage, education, and names of everyone in the family. For instance, the 1910 census includes Civil War veteran tallies. The 1900 census records the birth places of everyone's parents. The 1920 census records how many children were born to the parents of the home and how many of those children are still living. Today most information that genealogists find interesting about persons' lives are no longer recorded in censuses.

You can follow an ancestor's life through the ten-year snapshots that censuses provide. Most research databases have specific strategies and advice for finding your ancestors through census searches. It is a great way to begin your family research.

Here is a QR link to a page on the United States Census website that shows the census records of well-known Americans. QR code readers can be found in app stores for free. Once downloaded, you open the app and hover the camera over the QR codes for a specific action. The ones I created for this book open websites.

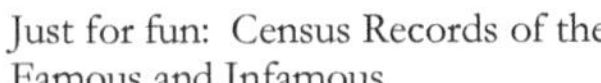
Just for fun: Census Records of the Famous and Infamous

Chapter 3: Everyone Has a Family, the U.S. Census

On this page are clips from the 1900 U. S. census of Joshua's family. (The entire page has much more detail about their education, occupation, and home). A census was recorded by a neighbor hired to record, or enumerate information and to verify the number of people in each home so that there would be correct representation in United States Congress. Each census unveils bits of information about the family. I labeled the parts that will be helpful. Write down what you discover. The blank form will help.

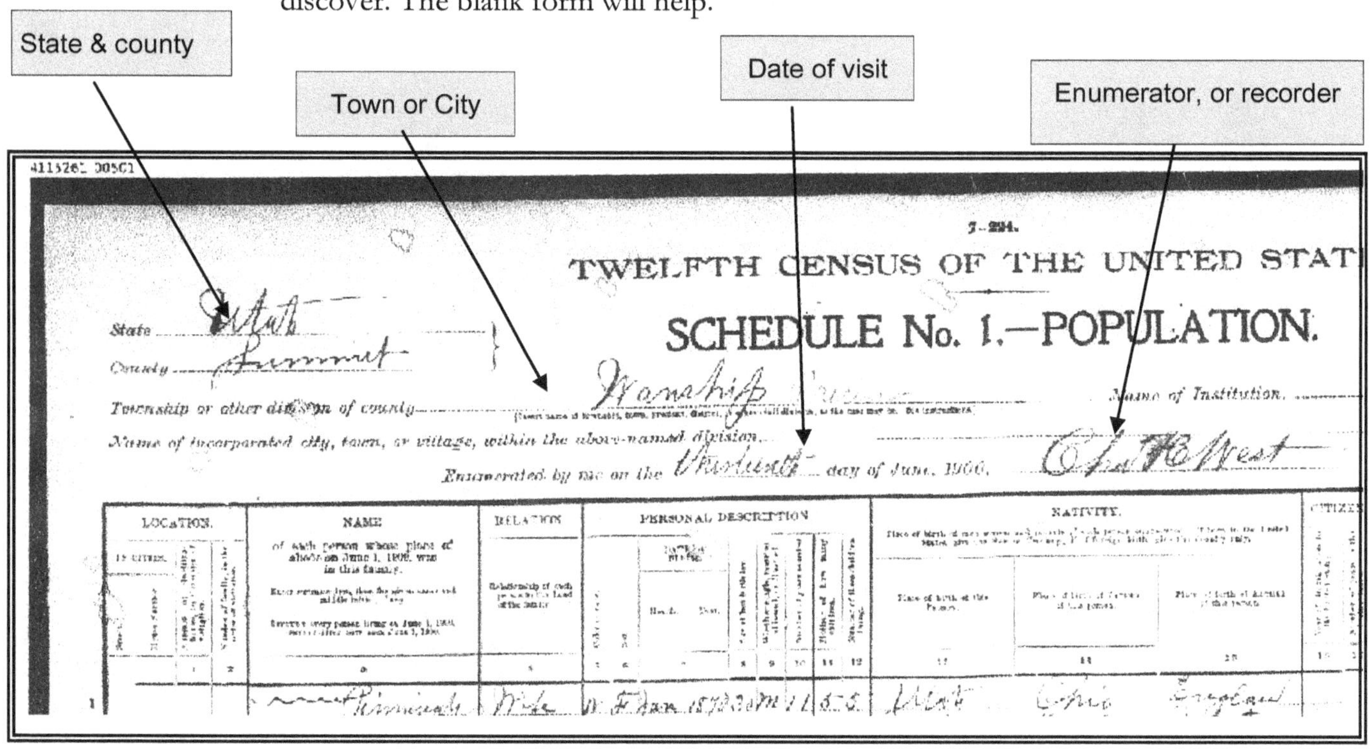

	103	~~ Millie	Dau	W	F	June	1887	12	S					Utah
99	103	Martin Reynold	Head	W	M	Mar	1829	71	M	35	5			Engl
		~~ Jane	Wife	W	F	June	1839	60	M	35	5	2		Eng
100	104	Bates Joshua	Head	W	M	Apr	1869	31	M	6	–	–		Utah
		~~ Eliza	Wife	W	F	Nov	1872	27	M	6	2	2		Utah
		~~ Joshua H	Son	W	M	Apr	1895	5	S					Utah
		~~ Andrew P	Son	W	M	July	1898	1	S					Utah
101	105	Lars Heeniz	Head	W	M	Jan	1814	83	M	15				Engl

Do your best to read this. The films from which these come are hard to read also. This information was recorded _____________ years ago!

Here is a chunk of the 1910 Wanship census record. What has changed in the Bates Family?

____

____

LOCATION.		NAME	RELATION.	PERSONAL DESCRIPTION				
Number of dwelling house in order of visitation.	Number of family in order of visitation.	of each person whose place of abode on April 15, 1910, was in this family. Enter surname first, then the given name and middle initial, if any. Include every person living on April 15, 1910. Omit children born since April 15, 1910.	Relationship of this person to the head of the family.	Sex.	Color or race.	Age at last birthday.	Whether single, married, widowed, or divorced.	Number of years of present marriage.
1	2	3	4	5	6	7	8	9
43	45	[illegible] Lyle R.	Head	M	W	34	M1	9
		—— Bertha A.	Wife	F	W	29	M1	9
		—— James B.	Son	M	W	8	S	
		—— Lyle R.	Son	M	W	6	S	
		—— Edgar L.	Son	M	W	4	S	
		—— Earl E.	Son	M	W	10/12	S	
44	46	Peterson Mary L.	Head	F	W	59	M2	
44	47	Powell Albert J.	Head	M	W	27	M1	2
		—— Inez T.	Wife	F	W	22	M1	2
		—— Virginia [illegible]	Daughter	F	W	2	S	
		—— Jenkyn E.	Son	M	W	3/12	S	
45	48	Long Alice	Head	F	W	87	M2	
46	49	Bates Joshuah	Head	M	W	41	M1	16
		—— Eliza	Wife	F	W	37	M1	16
		—— Joshuah H.	Son	M	W	15	S	
		—— Andrew P.	Son	M	W	11	S	
		—— Roy R.	Son	M	W	7	S	
		—— Dorothy M.	Daughter	F	W	2	S	

1900 U.S. Census Form

1910 U.S. Census Form

Chapter 4: Reading Family Data Charts

Access to a blank Family Group Sheet

This chapter investigates the "family group sheet", a graphic organizer of a family of parents, their children, and basic data about each person. Children are listed oldest to youngest.

The best way to become acquainted with a family group sheet is to complete one for your family. You should know much of the information. Ask relatives for any information you need. Use your smart phone to scan the QR code to find the blank family group record. If you have set up printing from your phone, print a copy. Husband and wife come first. How you fill out the record depends on whether you place yourself as the husband, wife or as a child.

Data to include on any family group record:

- Full names (Maiden for wife)
- Birth dates
- Birth locations
- Male/Female
- Religion
- Occupation
- Religious ceremonies
- Spouse
- Marriage dates
- Marriage locations
- Death dates
- Cause of death
- Death locations
- Burial dates
- Burial locations
- Other marriages

Now investigate the family group sheet for Joshua and Eliza Bates' family to find out more specific information about Joshua H. Bates.

1. What is his rank in the births?
2. What specific information do you find?
3. Did he marry?
4. When did he die?
5. Where did he die?
6. How is this record different from the census?

Answers:

Joshua and Eliza Bates Family Group Record

HUSBAND BATES, Joshua

Born 26 Apr 1869 Place Wanship, Summit, Utah

Chr. Place

Marr. 6 June 1894 Place Wanship, Summit, Utah

Died 3 Aug 1958 Place Vancouver, Clark, Wash

Bur. 7 Aug 1958 Place Wanship, Summit, Utah

HUSBAND'S FATHER BATES, John HUSBAND'S MOTHER BROOKS, Margaret

HUSBAND'S OTHER WIVES

Husband BATES, Jos

Wife PETERSEN, E

Ward 1.

Examiners: 2.

Stake or Mission Ben Lomond

WIFE PETERSEN, Eliza

Born 8 Nov 1872 Place Wanship, Summit, Utah

Chr. Place

Died 11 June 1946 Place Wanship, Summit, Utah

Bur. 14 June 1946 Place Wanship, Summit, Utah

WIFE'S FATHER PETERSEN, Andrew WIFE'S MOTHER DABELSTEIN, Caroline Dorthea

WIFE'S OTHER HUSBANDS

	SEX M F	CHILDREN List Each Child (Whether Living or Dead) in Order of Birth SURNAME (CAPITALIZED) GIVEN NAMES	WHEN BORN DAY MONTH YEAR	WHERE BORN TOWN	COUNTY	STATE OR COUNTRY	DATE OF FIRST MARRIAGE TO WHOM	WHEN DIED DAY MONTH YEAR
1	M	BATES, Joshua Henry	2 Apr 1895	Wanship	Summit	Utah	unmd	4 Oct 1918
2	M	BATES, Andrew Parley	10 July 1898	Wanship	Summit	Utah	22 June 1921 LAMBERT, Lucille Roene	
3	M	BATES, Roy Richard	17 Feb 1903	Wanship	Summit	Utah	6 June 1923 HALLSTROM, Olive	
4	F	BATES, Dorothy Marie	12 July 1907	Wanship	Summit	Utah		28 Aug 1910
5	F	BATES, Effie Lucille	2 Jan 1911	Wanship	Summit	Utah	10 Aug 1933 WILDE, Leland	22 Nov 1946
6	M	BATES, Lorenzo John	29 Oct 1913	Wanship	Summit	Utah	26 Aug 1933 FERNELIUS, Laure Leone	
7	F	BATES, Ruth Margaret	5 Aug 1916	Wanship	Summit	Utah	11 Aug 1935 BRINTON, Dilworth	
8								
9								
10								
11								

SOURCES OF INFORMATION

Records of A. Parley Bates
North Ogden, Utah

2. Birth; bpt, marr certs

(1)

OTHER MARRIAGES

#7 Ruth md (2) 26 Mar 1964 to
YOUNG, Simeon Allyn

Chapter 5: Everyone Has a Family: Photographs

Who are the people in this photograph? Hint: Study the chart in Chapter 4.

Costuming websites give clues about how people dressed in different time periods.

Back row Left ______________________

Back Row Center ______________________

Back Row Right ______________________

Front Row Left ______________________

Front Row Bow/Hair ______________________

Front Row Round Collar______________________

Front Row in Lap ______________________

Front Row Right ______________________

See a problem with this photograph?

What is it? What happened? ______________________

What is most important about a photograph?

Guess the person,
Guess the age:

Left:
Name ____________
Age ________
Middle:
Name ____________
Age ________
Right:
Name ____________
Age ________

Photography Clues:
What is a "cabinet card" photo?

Name _______________
Age ________

Persons who label photographs are so appreciated by their grandchildren or great-grandchildren who would otherwise have no clue as to who is in the photograph!

Look at the back of the photograph with the three BOYS. Yes, all of them were boys. Are your answers the same as on the back of the photograph?

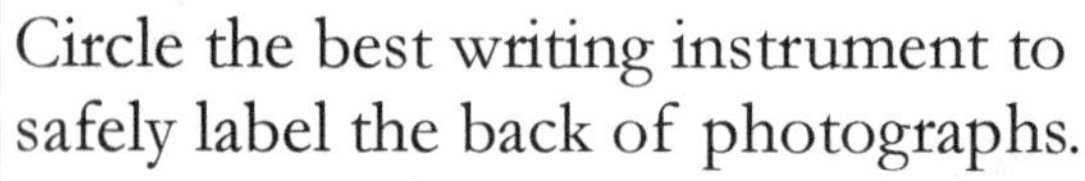

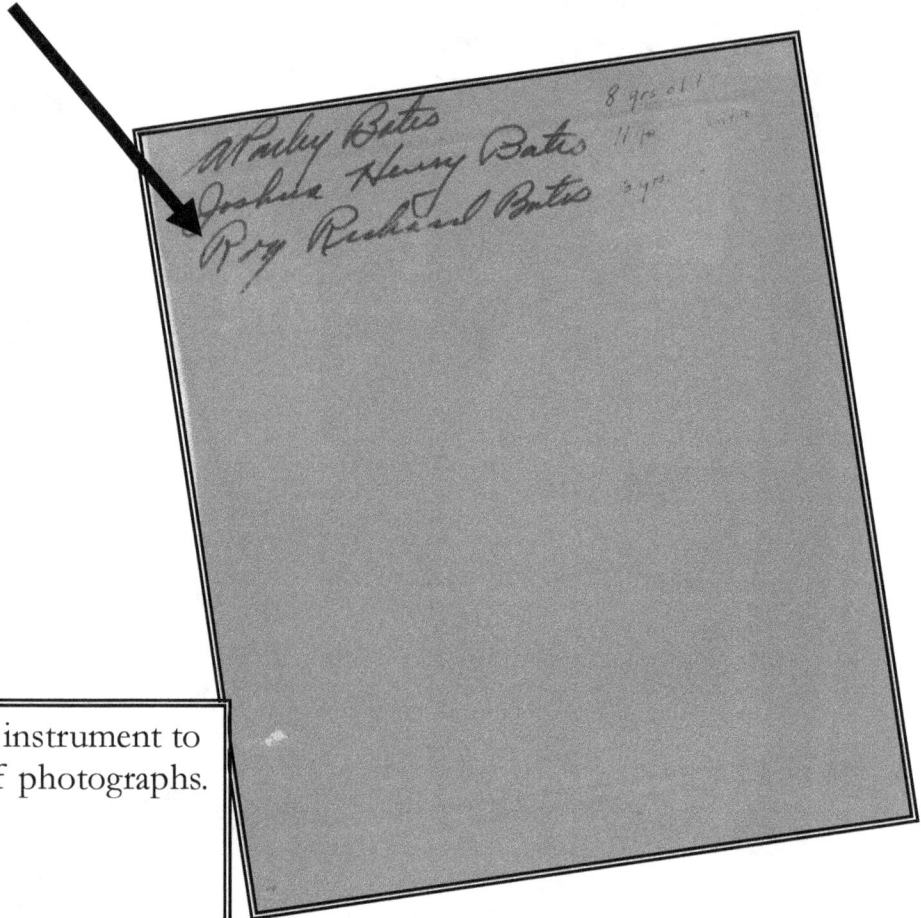

Circle the best writing instrument to safely label the back of photographs.

A. Soft-lead pencil
B. Mechanical pencil
C. Ballpoint pen
D. Permanent marker
E. Felt tip pen
F. Soft-tip, permanent marker
G. Applied labels

Photography labeling article

Family records and labeling help everyone detect "Who *is* that in the photograph?"

What about the backgrounds? Look again at all three photographs in this chapter, and write down what you see in the backgrounds.

Photograph	Background	Observations	Hypotheses
Entire Family			
Three Boys			
Toddler			

Backgrounds

Hairstyles

Chapter 6: What Photographs Reveal

Photographs reveal more than identities of their subjects. The QR codes at the end of Chapter 5 are links to a study of backdrops, dress and hairstyles. All can be clues when dating the photographs. If you are lucky enough to have photographs of people conducting their everyday life, you can piece together the clues in those photograph to learn more about what they did. Then one can draw a hypothesis about the photograph.

Tips to organize photos

No names are on the reverse side. But you can hypothesize as to who the subjects of the photograph are. Use the chart and censuses of previous chapters for reference.

Use the chart on the next page to analyze this photograph.

Online storage: Pinterest

All this emphasis on photographs begs me to ask how you store your photographs? Scan these QR code links to determine what might be the best storage strategies for yourself. You do not want grandchildren and great grandchildren to not know your

Online storage: Instagram

Create your own storage with WordPress.

Perfecting Detection Skills...Clues in Family Photographs

Describe what you see? What is the first thing you see? What people and objects do you see? What is the setting?

Identify the people in the photograph.

Who is the intended audience?

What can you learn from this image? Can you estimate the year?

Create a title, caption and summary for this photograph.

What do you wonder about?

What information does this photograph add about the family?

Chapter 7: Records of Joshua's Youth

Outside of photographs and family group charts there is often very little about children in genealogical records. Why do you think that is still the case?

____

____

How will your descendants become acquainted with you? What is important to keep from your childhood and your youth for a future record of yourself?

Materials that you might consider come under four major categories:

1. **Your physical appearance**
2. **What you say and write**
3. **What you do**
4. **What others say about you**

What are your records that would contribute to your life story? Fill out anything you think of and add items later.

1. ______________________________________
2. ______________________________________
3. ______________________________________
4. ______________________________________
5. ______________________________________
6. ______________________________________
7. ______________________________________

A SPLENDID AUDIENCE

Greeted the Eighth Grade Graduates Monday Evening Last--Wholesome Advice Imparted--Diplomas

It was a s
was present at
moncement e
The Dewey th
front to back w
friends of the
bright boys a
County who r
ing them to e
commencement
As the curta
presented was
one--as to the
capable high
happy faces of
arrayed in "th
vealed to the
audience. An
greeted the g
teachers.
County Sup
Cooper acted a
and announced
fine a program
tened to at a
After an inv
D. Lewis, the
to a fine pia
Grace Lawrence
It was cleverly
siastically recei
Superintenden
gave the addre
was a splendid
held the close
graduating clas
ence. He gave
vice to the gr
impressive ma
of this capable
The response
pal C. A. Whi
very pleasing
Miss Belva M
sang a solo, a
Fawn Sharps
was clever and
was demanded.
The graduatin

The graduating address was made by Mr. Orson Ryan of Salt Lake. He is an able speaker and held the closest attention of the class and audience. He is pruod of the fact that he is a Summit county boy, and Summit county in turn is proud of him, for he is a capable, learned gentleman.

Mrs. Ethel Lewis sang a solo in her usual pleasing manner and was enthusiastically recalled.

Then followed the presentation of the certificates by Superintendent Cooper, the names of those receiving them follows:

Henefer District No. 1—Ethel Beard Florence Beard.

Coalville District No. 2 —Leonard Willoughby, Warren Salmon, John T. Diston, Freddie Clark, Ethel Arnold, Enid Ruff, Eunice Calderwood, Wesley Randall, Alex Gilchrist, Hazel Wright, Willard Wilde, Lydia Deming, Cora Hopkin, Florence Taggart, Bayard Taylor, Gladys Wilde, David Wilde, David Johnson, Ethel Morton Jessie Johnson, Verna Fewkes.

Hoytsville District No. 3— Leo Wooley, Mabel Sargent, Byron Winters, Ivan Crittenden, Klea Gunn.

Wanship District No. 4— Joshua H. Bates.

Peoa District No. 6—Leroy Marchant, Pheren Maxwell Leroy Roos, Irvin Maxwell, Grace Wright, Sarah Jorgensen, Ivie Marchant.

Kamas District No.7–Tommy Parry Bernard Williams, Ralph Park, Madaline McCormick, Eva Benson, Parley Lambert, Vernettie Williams, Lilith Pitt, Virgil King, Ivie Gines.

Parley's Park District No. 9— Pearl Wabel, Addie Johnson.

Park City District No. 12 — Noel Phillips, Edith Nancarrow, Frank Carrigan, Blanche Thompson, Emma Thompson, Katie Cloonan, Florence McCarthy, Grace Lawrence, Nina Reynolds, Mary Abbey, Nellie M. O'Neil, Wm. Whitis, Thomas Berbeck, Catherine Towey, Victoria Furter, Irone Marchant, Philip Rall, Jean Bonnie, Jennie Thomas, George Gidley, Edith McFarland, Wm. R. Blackler, Marion Dunbar, Harry Raddon, Mildred Konold, Olive Allen.

Oakley District No. 13—Cecil Peterson, Pearl Franson, Clarence R. Frazier, William Franson, Charles English, Fannie Page, Lillie Hallstrum, Carl Horton, Leona Louder.

Echo District No. 15—Ruth Toone, F. T. Wilson, Stanley Wilson.

Write the information you discover about Joshua H. Bates in this newspaper article from the *Park Record*, June 3, 1914.

____

____

Joshua's life orbited around four hubs: family, church, school and friends.

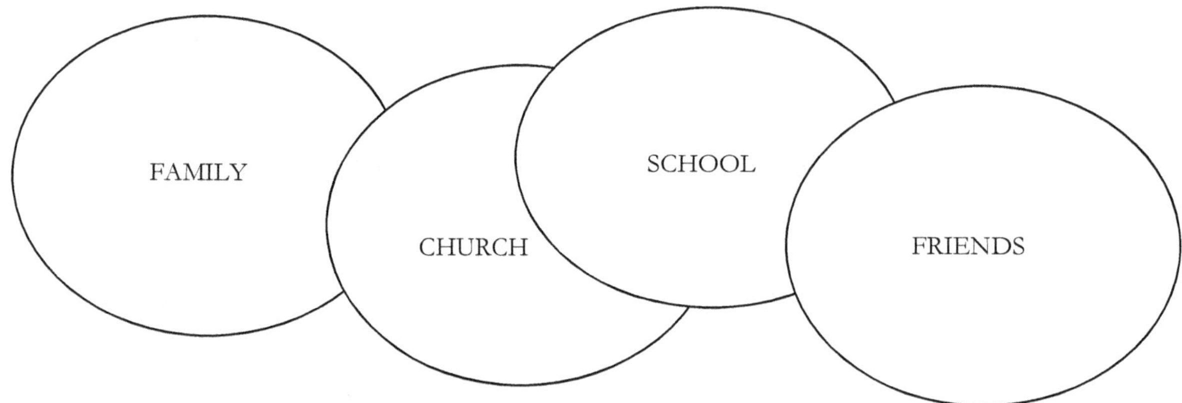

What kind of records could each of theses hubs create about Joshua? Brainstorm possible records and write each in the appropriate circle above.

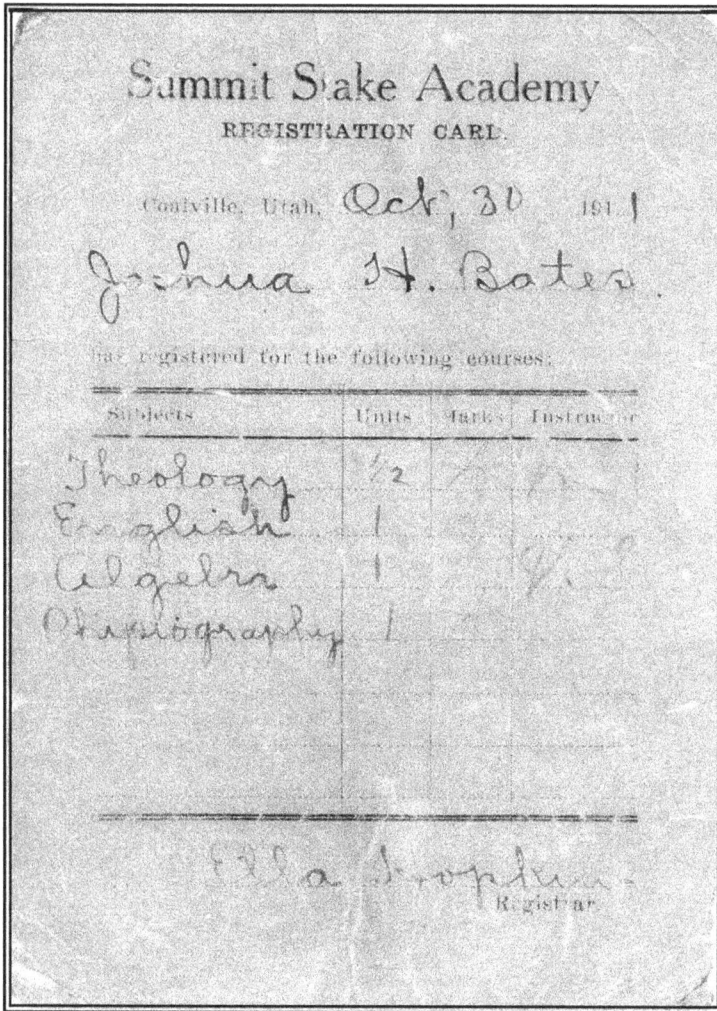

Summit Stake Academy

REGISTRATION CARD

Coalville, Utah, Oct, 30 1911

Joshua H. Bates

has registered for the following courses:

Subjects	Units	Marks	Instructor
Theology	1/2		
English	1		
Algebra	1		
Orthography	1		

Ella [illegible]

Registrar

Record Source: *School*

Title of record: ______________________________

Date of record: __________

Information about Joshua in this record: ______________________________

Summit Stake Academy

REGISTRATION CARD.

Coalville, Utah, Oct. 8, 1912

Joshua H. Bates

has registered for the following courses:

Subjects	Units	Marks	Instructor
Theology b	½	97	Case
English b	1	93	Case
Math b	1	97	
Hist a	1	95	Case
Drawing	½	80	E. L.
Manual T	½	97	V. D.

C. A. White
Registrar.

Record Source: ____________________

Title of record:

____

____

Date of record: __________

Information about Joshua in this record:

____

____

____

____

____

____

Record Source: ____________________

Title of record:

____

____

Date of record: __________

Information about Joshua in this record:

____

____

____

____

____

____

Summit Stake Academy

REGISTRATION CARD.

Coalville, Utah, April 13, 1912

Joshua H. Bates

has registered for the following courses:

Subjects	Units	Marks	Instructor
Theology	½	A	V. S.
Algebra	1	A	V. S.
English	1	A	White
Physiography	1	A	White

Registrar.

Record Source: ______________________

Title that I would give to the record:

____

____

First date of record: __________

Last date of record: __________

Information about Joshua in this record:

____

____

____

____

____

____

____

____

____

Name. Joshua H. Bates
Where Born. Wanship, Utah
Date of Birth April 2, 1895
Father's Name Joshua Bates
Mother's Maiden Name Eliza Petersen
When Blessed June 6, 1895
By Whom Ebenezer R. Young
When Baptized Aug. 15, 1903
By Whom Frank D. Hixon
When Confirmed Aug 16, 1903
By Whom Henry Reynolds
Ordained Deacon Feb 2, 1908
By Wm Crook
Ordained Teacher Feb 12 1912
By Alma Gibbons

BACK

FRONT

Coalville, Utah Nov 26 1916

To the Presidency of the 5 Elders' Quorum of the Summit Stake of Zion,

DEAR BRETHREN:

This Certifies that, at a Stake Priesthood Meeting held at Wanship on the 26 day of Nov, 1916, Brother Joshua H. Bates was recommended by his bishop as being worthy of being ordained an Elder. Said recommend was approved by the Stake priesthood. You will please see that he is ordained, and received a member in your Quorum.

[illegible] Stake Clerk

School Photograph, Wanship, Utah

Probable ID:
To estimate the year and Joshua's age, look at this article to decide what school is behind the students.
Year______ Age _______
Probable ID:
Probable ID:

No. 61 **REGISTRATION CARD** Oct. 13 1913-14

NORTH HIGH SCHOOL DISTRICT OF SUMMIT COUNTY, UTAH

Admit Joshua H. Bates of Wanship Utah

To the following Classes: 3rd Year.

First Semester	Unit	1st mo.	2nd mo.	3rd mo.	4th mo.	1st Sem.	Second Semester	Unit	5th mo.	6th mo.	7th mo.	8th mo.	2nd Sem.
Engl C	1/2		A	A		A	Engl C	1/2	A-	A			A
Amer Hist	1/2	a	a	A+		a	Civics [illegible]	1/2	—				a
Rural Econ	1/2	B+	A	A-		A-	Physiology	1/2					
Oral Exp	1/4		A-	A-		A-	Oral Exp	1/4	B+	B+			a
Music	1/4			[illegible]		B+	Music	1/4	B+	B+			B+
							Elem. Agri	1	a	a	a		a

Approved .... Principal *Approved* .... Principal

REGISTRATION CARD

North Summit High School Sept 8 1914

ADMIT Bates, Joshua *to the following classes*

English D
Algebra B
Solid Geometry
Ancient History
Physics
Physiology B.

J. M. Cummings *Principal*

Above Record Source:

____

Title of record:

____

Date of record: __________

Information about Joshua in this record:

____

____

____

____

____

____

____

____

____

____

____

____

How can I organize primary sources about me?

ONE. BOX.

In that box have slim file folders for each year of your life. Include the best photos, the best art, the best programs, the best certificates, all documents that record events in your life, and mementos you truly would miss.

Only rule: everything has to comfortably fit in the slim file folders.

Preserving paper items: Place in sheet protectors with one sheet of copy paper, both have archival properties.

W 6797
Rigby . 1758R.

BOARD OF EDUCATION OF NORTH SUMMIT SCHOOL DISTRICT

P. H. NEELEY....................PRESIDENT
T. J. LEWIS...............VICE PRESIDENT
ALMA GIBBONS
ELMER WRIGHT
GEORGE P. JONES
C. R. JONES ....Clerk of Board
G. HOWARD BEARD..... Treasurer of Board

Board of Education of North Summit High School

P. H. NEELEY.....................President
ALFRED JONES .... Vice President
ALONZO WINTERS.......................Clerk
GEORGE P. JONES............ .....Treasurer
W. D. BROWN
ALMA GIBBONS
ELMER WRIGHT
JOSEPH S. BALL
J L. KEARNS.... ...County Superintendent

FACULTY

J. M. CUMMINGS.......................Principal
W. R. SHARP
MARGUERITE S. CAMERON
B. F. LOFGREEN
ALICE L. ELDER

Commencement Exercises
OF
THE CLASS OF 1915
North Summit High School
IN
SUMMIT STAKE TABERNACLE

MAY TWENTY-SEVENTH NINETEEN HUNDRED FIFTEEN

At 8 O'clock p. m.

How old was Joshua when he graduated from high school? ___

Name of high school? ___________

Ideas about why he was this age? ___________

____

____

GRADUATES

WILFORD N. SARGENT
JOSHUA H. BATES
KLEA M. GUNN
HAZEL WRIGHT
FRED A. REES
FRANK J. REES
CORA HOPKIN
J. WARREN SALMON
AFFRA PETTIT
VALLIERE BALL
GLENN BEARD

PROGRAM

"JUNE"........................School Chorus

Invocation

"Madeline"......................School Chorus

Salutatory..................Wilford N. Sargent

Reading........................Affra Pettit

"Juanita".......................Male Chorus

Address...................Prof. F. W. Reynolds

Valedictory....................Joshua H. Bates

Presentation of Diplomas......Pres. P. H. Neeley

"Blow Bugle Blow"...............School Chorus

Benediction

How large was the graduating class? ___________

What was Joshua's role at the graduation ceremony?

____

____

Insights: Cursive Writing

If reading cursive is challenging, consider trying these strategies. I do know this: you will become proficient with practice. It is just like practicing throwing free throws, you get better.

1. If a word is difficult, skip it. Read the rest of the sentence and see if the context of the sentence helps you with the mystery word. It also helps to remember that cursive writing just connects the letters of a word.
2. Another tip: Joshua often writes *d, g, p, s* and *a* opened instead of closed.

3. Look at capital and lower case alphabets for the general time period. Depending on the time, the alphabets wildly differ.

British Round Hand

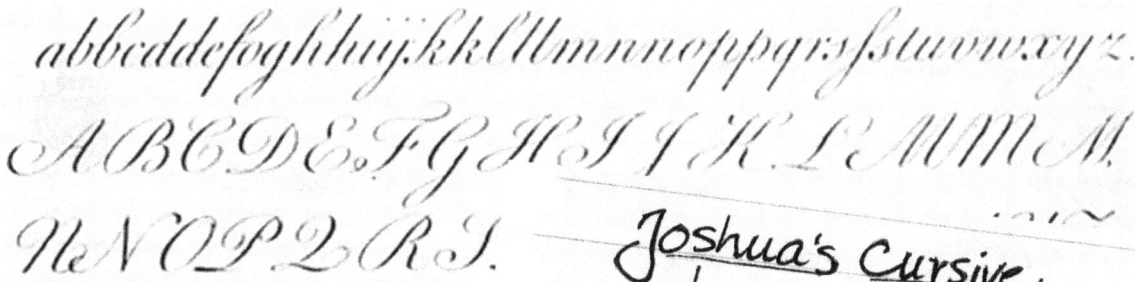

Palmer Method

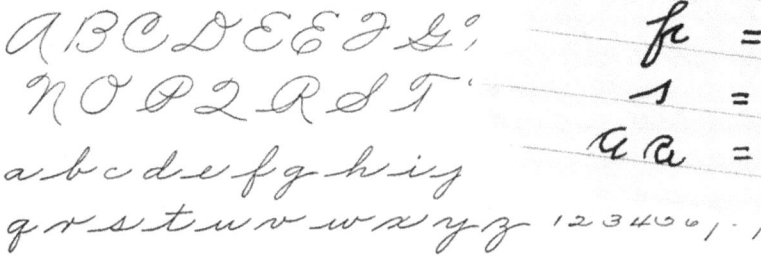

Joshua's Cursive

= d bed

= p play

= s calves

= a halls

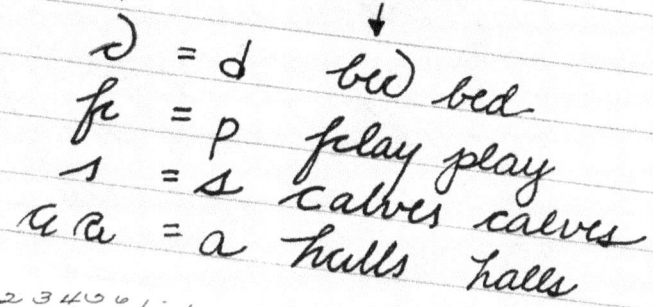

3. Linking printed letters: Print a simple sentence. Then go back to each word and link each letter in the word with a line that flow logically from the last stroke of one letter to the beginning stroke of another. This will give you a feel for cursive and perhaps help in writing more cursive yourself.

4. Air tracing: using your index finger as a pen, trace the mystery letter or word in the air. I use this often when transcribing old documents.

5. Paper tracing or copying: This is similar, but you trace with a real writing implement on scratch paper and see if by replicating the movement and shape of the letters you discover the letters.

Chapter 8: Joshua's Journal Begins: The Title Page

Journal of
Joshua H. Bates
Wanship, Utah.
Born April 2, 1895
Diary begun April 2, 1916.

Please yourself and do your duty as you see it.

Act natural, be yourself.

When you do a thing make it go.

Pleasure is not all there is in life but enjoy yourself.

When your chance comes take it, it soon passes probably never to return.

Do not talk to hear your own voice when speaking have a purpose and make your ~~yo~~ words as few as will convey the meaning.

Why did Joshua start a journal *now*?

What could motivate you to journal?

Transcription:

Transcribe (copy *exactly* as written). Then share your conclusions about:

1. why Joshua started his journal now,
2. what evidence proves that conclusion,
3. what this journal title page divulges about Joshua's personality.

Chapter 9: University Days

Being the protector, patriarch and provider of families, it was important for young men to find a way to earn money. In 1910, only 19.9% (two of ten) of all women over 16 years of age in the United States worked for wages outside the home (InfoPlease). In Utah that translated to 118,100 men employed and only 18,400 women employed (Historical). Joshua farmed and ranched with his father, but trained for a different vocation.

Transcribe (copy as written, no corrections) the following four journal excerpts about his University of Utah days.

Mon. Up to the University and
June 12 register for summer school in the
forenoon in the afternoon I go
out to Uncle Freds place to a
couple of shows at night with
Everett

Journal, June 12, 1916, p.12.

Thursday To school all day home and out to
June 15 dance at Saltair at night a good time
home & to-bed by 12:00.

Journal, June 15, 1916, p. 13.

University of Utah, circa 1920

Friday June 16. To school. The faculty give the summer students a reception in the afternoon. Rather a formal affair not a very good time. Home at 5:30 in at night.

Journal, June 16, 1916, p. 13.

Mon June 19 To school all day.

Tues. 20. To school all day home at night

Wednesday June 21 To school al day home at night

Thursday School all day

Friday June 23 To school all day. To picture show at night.

Journal, June 19-23, 1916, p. 14.

Month:

Main activity:

Forms about Joshua's choice of occupation are in this chapter. Look at each one for clues about his chosen occupation. Then record the title, date, and significance of each document for Joshua on the last page of this chapter.

A.

STATE OF UTAH
DEPARTMENT OF PUBLIC INSTRUCTION
SALT LAKE CITY

Page
Month JUL 15 1915
Year

STATE BOARD OF EDUCATION
E. J. GOWANS, Chairman
J. T. KINGSBURY, Secretary
J. A. WIDTSOE
D. H. CHRISTENSEN
C. R. MARCUSEN

Name Joshua H. Bates

In the recent county teachers' examination given by the State Board of Education you obtained the following grades:

Writing 80	*U. S. History* 90	*Drawing* 53
Spelling 91	*Physiology* 80	*Psychology* 80
Arithmetic 61	*Geography* 82	*History of Education* 50
Grammar 64	*Reading* 82	*Educational Book*
Pedagogy 68	*Nature Study* 70	*Average*

According to the regulations of the State Board an applicant for a certificate must receive an average of 70 per cent, and must not fall below 50 per cent in any subject. New applicants to teachers' examination are not required to pass examination in the home reading books. This examination is for teachers who desire to renew subjects in which they have a grade of eighty per cent from the 1914 examination. Teachers who have had three years' successful teaching experience are not required to pass examination in Psychology and History of Education.

E. G. GOWANS,
Chairman State Board of Education.

B.

No. 7221

University of Utah

Salt Lake City, Jan 8, 1916

Received from Joshua Bates

the sum of ~~Twelve~~ Ten *Dollars, Registration Fee for the Year.*

~~$12.00~~ 10 correspondence D. R. Allen

Secretary

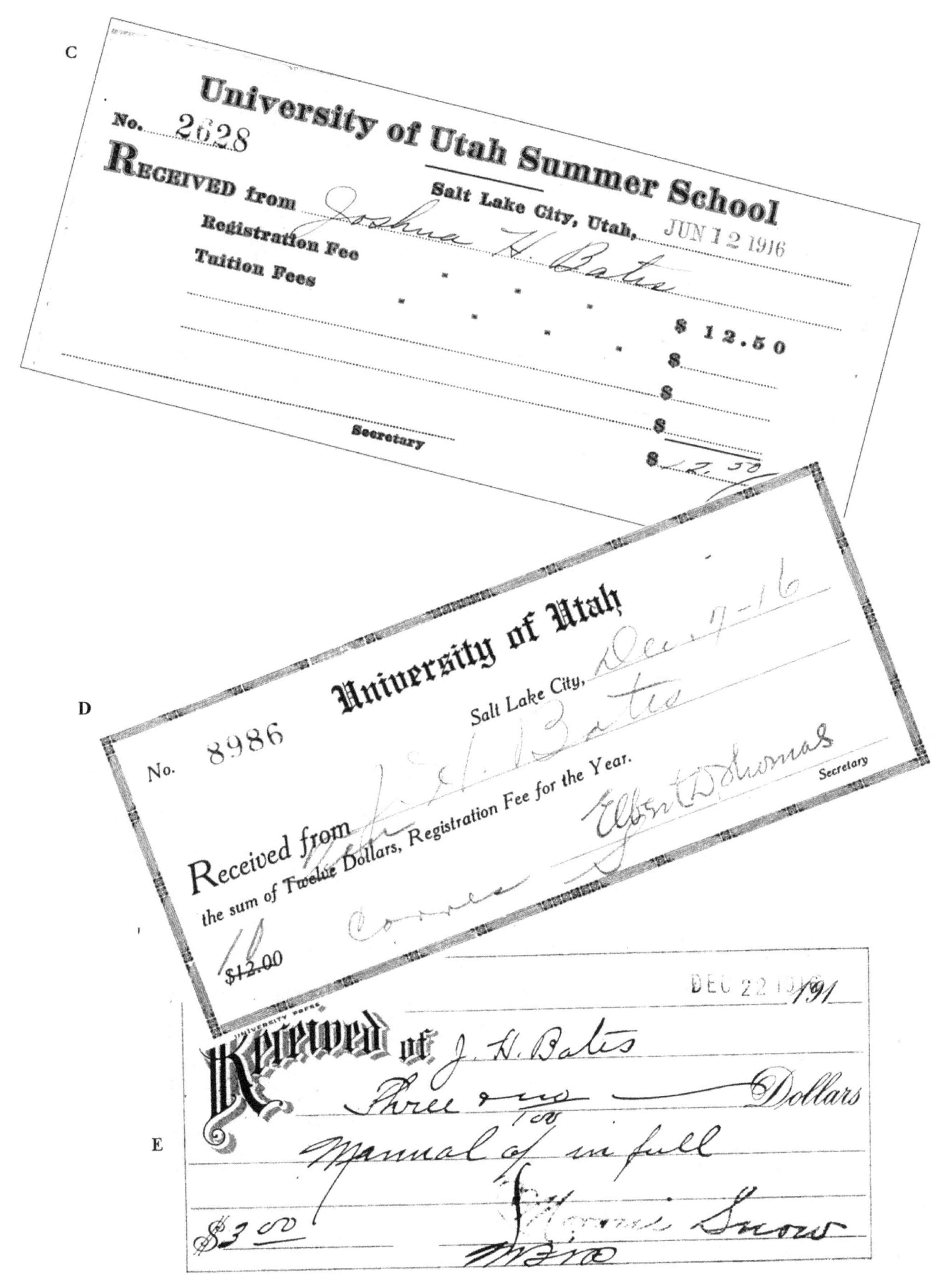

C

University of Utah Summer School

No. 2628

Salt Lake City, Utah, JUN 12 1916

RECEIVED from Joshua H. Bates

Registration Fee . . . . $ 12.50

Tuition Fees . . . . $

$

$

Secretary $ 12.50

D

University of Utah

No. 8986

Salt Lake City, Dec 7-16

Received from J. H. Bates

the sum of ~~Twelve~~ Dollars, Registration Fee for the Year.

Corres

Elbert D. Thomas
Secretary

~~$12.00~~ 10

E

DEC 22 1916 191

Received of J. H. Bates

Three $\frac{no}{100}$ Dollars

Manual of in full

$3 00

Morris Snow

F.

State of Utah

Department of Public Instruction

Salt Lake City

State Board of Education

E. G. GOWANS, Chairman J. T. KINGSBURY, Secretary
J. A. WIDTSOE D. H. CHRISTENSEN C. R. MARCUSEN

County Teacher's Certificate

This Certifies, *That* JOSHUA H. BATES *having given evidence of possessing the required qualifications, is authorized according to law to teach in the Elementary Grades of the Public Schools of the State of Utah, until June 30, 1917.*

Issued at Salt Lake City, Utah, AUGUST 3, *1916.*

E. G. Gowans
Chairman of the State Board of Education

THE F. W. GARDINER CO. PRESS, SALT LAKE 87126

G

State of Utah

Department of Public Instruction

Salt Lake City.

State Board of Education

E. G. GOWANS, CHAIRMAN J. T. KINGSBURY, SECRETARY
J. A. WIDTSOE D. H. CHRISTENSEN C. R. MARCUSEN

Grammar Grade County Teacher's Certificate

August 14, 1915.

This Certifies, *That* JOSHUA H. BATES *known as a person of good moral character and having passed a satisfactory examination in the following subjects:* being

Writing, Arithmetic, Pedagogy, Physiology, Reading, Drawing, Orthography, English Grammar, U. S. History, Geography, Nature Study, Psychology and History of Education,

is authorized according to law to teach in the Grammar Grades of the Public Schools of the State of Utah. Valid until June 30, *191*6.

VOID UNLESS COUNTERSIGNED BY THE CHAIRMAN OF THE STATE BOARD OF EDUCATION

E. G. Gowans

H.

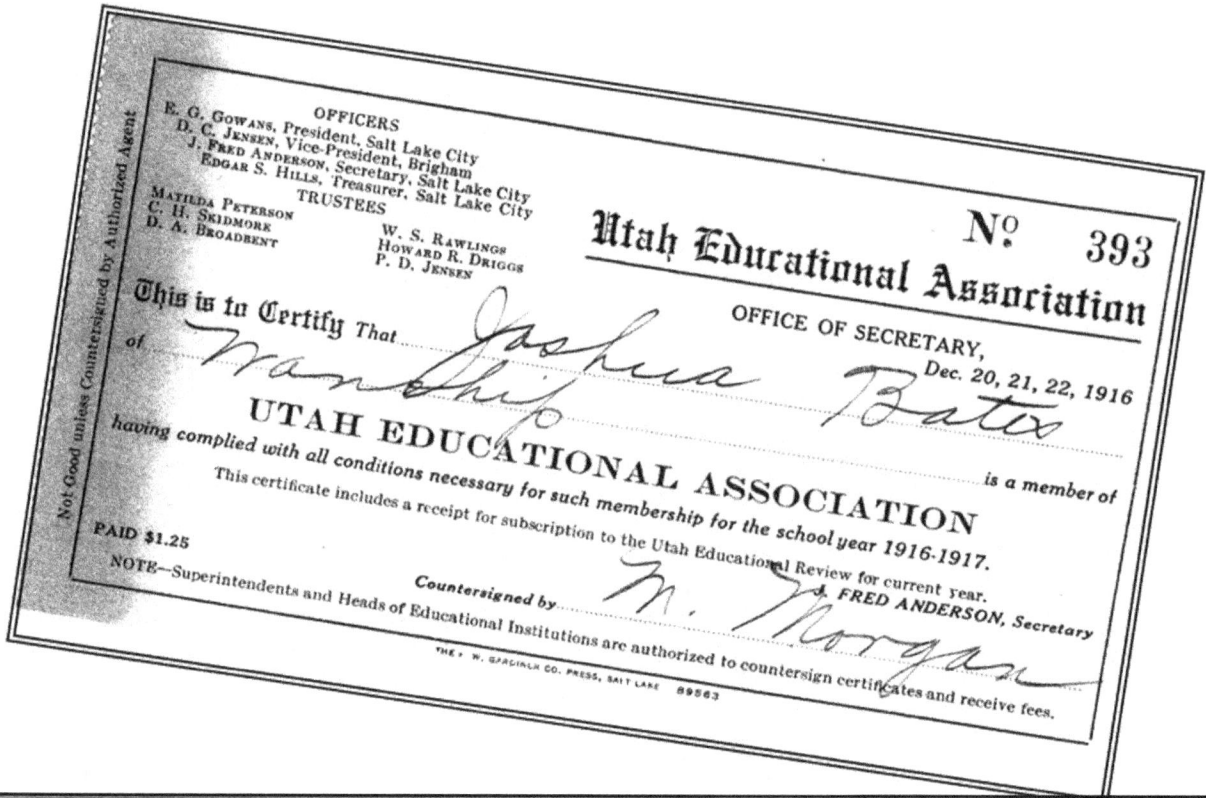

Not Good unless Countersigned by Authorized Agent

Nº 393

Utah Educational Association

OFFICE OF SECRETARY,
Dec. 20, 21, 22, 1916

This is to Certify That Joshua Bates
of Manship
having complied with all conditions necessary for such membership for the school year 1916-1917. is a member of

UTAH EDUCATIONAL ASSOCIATION

This certificate includes a receipt for subscription to the Utah Educational Review for current year.

PAID $1.25

J. FRED ANDERSON, Secretary

Countersigned by M. Morgan

NOTE—Superintendents and Heads of Educational Institutions are authorized to countersign certificates and receive fees.

THE F. W. GARDINER CO. PRESS, SALT LAKE 89563

Record the title, date, significance of each document for Joshua.

A.

B.

C.

D.

E.

F.

G.

H.

Chapter 10: On the Town

Young adulthood is an exhilarating time. You have just graduated from high school and are hoping that your decisions now will serve you well for the next 40 to 50 years!

In 1917, they danced, watched movies, enjoyed using telephones, played ball, and fell in love. Glaringly missing were smart phones, gaming, movies on demand, fitness watches and online gadgets of all varieties. How did they fill up their days? The this chapter and the following chapters illustrate the rich social lives of young adults of the time.

The median age for a first marriage in 1910 was 25.1 years for males and 21.6 for females, and in 1920 it was 24.6 for males and 21.2 for females. In comparison, in 2010 ages for marriage were 28.2 for males and 26.1 for females (http://www.infoplease.com/ipa.A0005061.html). Statistically speaking, marriage was a ways off for Joshua when he graduated from high school. So what was in store for him? Having a grand time dancing, singing, and watching picture shows! Here are some background photographs and descriptions of places that you will read about in Joshua's journal when he describes his social life.

Mecca of the Social Scene: Saltair

Passengers rode the Salt Lake, Garfield, and Western Railway, which went to and from Saltair every forty-five minutes, beginning at 9:30 am, to escape for a day of leisure at Saltair. The train ride itself was all part of the fun.
"Whole trains spontaneously burst into song."
Wallace Stegner, McCormick's *Saltair*

Dancers enjoy the sounds of a live band as they swoop around the roomy dance floor c. 1914.

The melodic Rhythm of R.Owen Sweeten's "Jazziferous Band" invigorated and energized the dancers of Saltair for seven years (1917 to 1924).

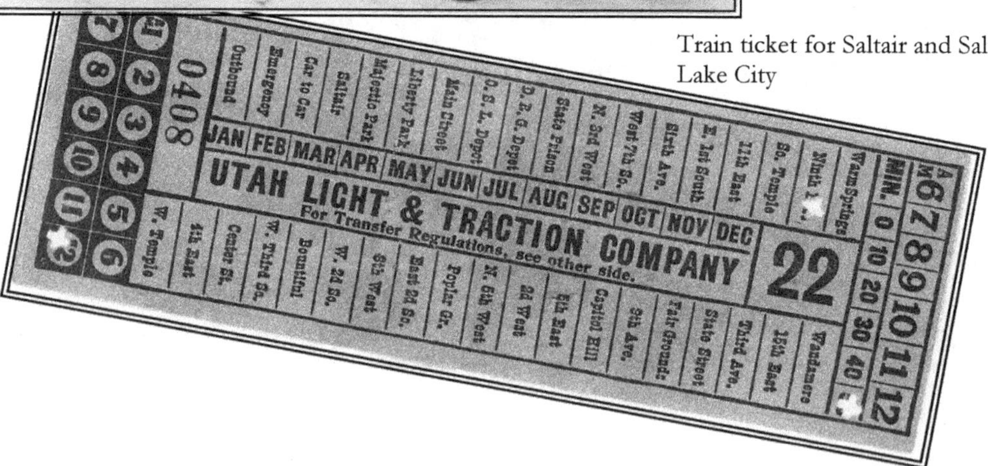

Train ticket for Saltair and Salt Lake City

Salt Lake Theatre

The Union Pacific Railroad donated electrical lamps to replace gas lamps.

The Grand Opera Theatre

Perfecting Detection Skills…On the Town

= 13 =

1916

Thursday June 15. To school all day home and out to dance at Saltair at night a good time home & to-bed by 12:00.

Friday June 16. To school. The faculty give the summer students a reception in the afternoon. Rather a formal affair not a very good time. Home at 5:30 in at night.

Saturday June 17. Up at 9:00. Dinner at 11: and then bath. Edd Young comes up and we go see the Birth of a Nation at the Salt Lake Theater. Certainly a great play. I think the greatest picture product ion I ever witnessed. We eat supper down town. After supper we went out to Majestic Park to a dance. Dance until about 11:00 then we ride up town and go into a Cafe until about a quarter of one then I catch my car home in bed at 1:15 & Don't sleep much very warm.

Sunday June 18. Home all day. Read the paper, sleep and loaf. Study and write on journal a night to bed at 10:30 not as warm as it was yesterday.

List the location Joshua went, with whom, and the activity:

=15=

Thursday June 29 — To school all day. Home at night study and to bed 10:15

Friday June 30. — To school all day. Out to Saltair at night have a good time. Met Mr Sharp out there and he made me acquainted with several of his lady friends.

Saturday July 1. — Home ~~all day~~ all day until I went out to see Clara; she seems quite glad to see me. Home and to dance at night.

Sunday July 2 — At home all day and read "Lepord Spots". In afternoon Ruth comes down to see Lisle and we spend the afternoon rather pleasantly. To bed early.

July 3. Monday — Home and read until afternoon when I go out to see uncle Fred's folks. they are going out to Wanship to spend the Fourth and wanted me to go with them but I would miss Wednesday school. To bed at 10:30

July 4 Tuesday. — Home until about 3:30 P.M. when I go down town go to a picture show and come home for supper eat supper and catch the 7:15 train for Saltair. There was a very large crowd. I meet Vinnie Rigby and Miss Kirk and some other girls. While talking to them

List each location to which Joshua went, with whom, and the activity:

=18=

Everett comes up. He does not care to dance so leaves for home on an early train. I dance with the girls until they leave then I have to make my way by "butting in," and meeting some people I already knew. Miss Craig & Miss Montgomery, Miss Duncan Miss Christensen, Miss, De Young, and others. Such a crowd that the regular trains could not accommodate us so I am forced to take the extra which struck Saltair Depot about 2:00 a.m. The Street car company had a special "lineup" at the depot so I took the Fifth avenue car right there home and in bed by 2:30 a good time on the whole.

Wednesday July 5. Up at 7:00 a.m. a little late to school but not the only one and several were not there at all. Home right after classes and sleep till supper time study at night. In bed at 10:

Thursday July 6. To school all day. Home and study at night. a bath and to bed by 10:30.

Friday. July 7. To school all day. Home in the afternoon and to a show at night. Have a good laugh

List each location to which Joshua went, with whom, and the activity:

Chapter 11: "Sweet on Someone"

Young men in the early twentieth century were gentlemanly and honorable. They enjoyed group social events including dances with live bands and many dance partners. This photograph of Joshua Bates and Rena Smith illustrates the restraint of the times....close, in proximity, but not touching, not even holding hands. This was after months of dating.

This chapter shows the growth of a relationship. Will you be able to tell when it started? Will you be able to gauge if all is well or if there are challenges?

Prompts will help you along the way. On your own paper reference your answers with the journal entry dates.

July 4. Tuesday. Home until about 3:30 P.M. when I go down town go to a picture show and came home for supper eat supper and catch the 7:15 train for Saltair. There was a very large crowd. I meet Vinnie Rigby and Miss Kirk and some other girls. While talking to them

Journal, Tuesday July 4, 1916, p. 15.

What is your interpretation of Josh's social connections? It there anyone special to him? How can you tell?

Everett comes up. He does not care to dance so leaves for home on an early train. I dance with the girls until they leave then I have to make my way by "butting in," and meeting some people I already knew. Miss Craig & Miss Montgomery, Miss Duncan, Miss Christensen, Miss De Young, and others. Such a crowd that the regular trains could not accommodate us so I am forced to take the extra which struck Saltair Depot about 2:00 A.M. The Streetcar company had a special "line up" at the depot so I took the Fifth avenue car right there home and in bed by 2:30 a good time on the whole.

Journal, Monday July 4, 1916, p. 16.

What characteristics do you see displayed in Josh at the dance? Comment about his transportation. problems that night.

See if someone is mentioned more than others in the upcoming journal entries.

Mon. July 10. To school all day. Home and press my clothes. Down to Rigby's after supper to take Rean to a Show but instead we spend the evening up to Sirkes with Dorus and his girl. Take a little walk and back to Rigby's and home & to bed 11:30

Journal, Monday July 10, 1916, p. 17.

Names mentioned in these excerpts:

the stage. Go up town with Sid back to Rigby's and meet Rena and go to Earls and Lyles. R & I go out to Claras and back I go to meet the stage but Parley has gone somewhere. I go home but he isn't there. I get ready and go to Rigby's for Rena. Phone to Uncle Freds and find Parley is in town but has gone up to a show with Pearl and Clara. Rena & I go up town to Auerbach's store and see Miss Nelson go out and find Bert and to a show, "Where are My Children"! Good moral play.

Saturday July 22, 1916. p. 20.

Sunday July 23 Up at 7:30 breakfast and go down town to meet Parley he is there and we go back up to Hissons. After dinner we went out to uncle Freds. He, Everett and I go up town and spend the afternoon walking around and to a show. I leave Parley + Everett down town and go home after supper I go up to Kirks to see Rena. The Bunch Rena, Vinnie Edith, Bert, Sid, and myself go down town to a show. after the show we go to the Palace and have some ice cream. ~~Home~~ Back to Kirks and then out to Uncle Freds to sleep in bed at 12:30

Journal, Sunday, July 23 , 1916, p. 22.

Names mentioned:

What you noticed:

: 25

for about half an hour. We go back to Rigleys and get the girls and from there go ~~the~~ to Saltairs to spend the rest of the day. Meet Bert + Stella and go in bathing. Dance at night. Home on the ~~eleven~~ 11:45 miss the line up and have to walk to Kirks. I walk back to Hissons and to bed by 2:00.

Journal, Monday July 24, 1916, p. 22.

= 23 =

Saturday July 28. To the farm and work on the ditch until noon. After-noon spent in turning hay. Home by six and get ready to go to show in Coalville. Pearly drives the car and R. and I set in the back seat. Show pretty good. Home and in bed by 12:00. R souvinere.

Sunday All knocked out this morning. I do

Journal, Saturday, day July 29, 1916, p. 23.

Guesses about what the souvenir (sovinere) could be?

I think a few things are cleared up in my mind at present future will tell. Have resolved on knowing a thing or two by or before the end of the week. Fore warned is fore armed and there is no cure like a preventitive.

Journal, Sunday August 13, 1916, p 25.

This is cryptic. What could be "cleared up" in his mind?

Friday 18 Work in hay all day. To Coalville
Aug 18. at night to a dance. Park City music
have a swell time. Miss Cohn was among
the best dancers. Home & to bed 2:00

Journal, Friday, August 18, 1916, p. 26.

What is different about this dance?

Christmas day and lots of snow and
cold weather. Over to Smiths for Christmas
Dinner. Have a little "conflab" after
dinner no anger on my part. Sid
Rena & I go to Park on train which
doesn't get in until four o'clock
up there by five. Saw Doris and

Journal, Monday, December 25, 1916, p. 47.

What could "a little conflab" be?

Tuesday Jan. 30 — To school all day very small school. Over to see R. at night. She is Tending Mrs Homers house. Home 11:30. Eventful night.

Wednesday Jan. 31 — Do not keep appointment at school to-day for first time. Get out of bed at noon. Set around Aunt Mary's until 3:30 P.M. then move for home. Mother says I've got the measles so must go to bed. R Comes over & sees me.

Thur. Feb. 1. — Bed all day not very sick scarcely broken out. R. comes out at [illegible]

Friday Feb 2. — "Some Looker" I Like a rather sore face sort of chap. R. Comes over.

Saturday Feb 3. — Bed all day. R comes over late in afternoon for few minuits. I not very sick but very weak

Journal, Tuesday, Jan 30 through Saturday Feb 3,1917, p. 53

Was the measles vaccine available in 1917?

Previously Josh mentions that school is cancelled because of the spread of measles. How do measles affect the relationship with Rena?

Looking at this page and the next page, how many days in a row did Rena come over?

See the last entry on the next page? What do you think the "lecture" was about and from whom?

More about measles

=54=

1917

Sunday Feb. 4. Bed all day. Reports of War with Germany. I hope they stay only reports and became nothing more. Rena comes over at night and talks quite awhile.

Monday Feb. 5. Up today for a couple of hours spend part of time in writing up journal "rather shaky." Rena comes over.

Tuesday Feb. 6. Up all day. Rena comes over at night.

Wednesday Feb. 7. Around all day can't read so don't know what to do with myself. R. comes over at night.

Thursday Feb. 8. Sid comes over in afternoon & we play checkers. Out for the first today for about fifteen minutes. R. comes over at night

Friday Feb. 9. Over to Smiths and Homers in the afternoon. Rena comes over at night.

Saturday Feb. 10. Read Book today "The Right of The Strongest." Over to Aunt Mary's Smiths & Homers. Ren is down with the measles.

Sunday Feb. 11. Press clothes straighten rooms and write in journal before dinner. Afternoon spent in visiting. Evening over to Homers to see Rena. Home 12:00 / Lecture Etc.

58

Sunday Mar. 4. To Sunday School, meeting and mutual. After mutual do something unexpected. Drop into Homer's. Rena gets some-what "peeved". Home 11:45

Monday Mar. 5. To school all day. Go to Smith's at night to practice Play. Home 11:30

Still I wonder.

Journal, Sunday & Monday, March 4-5, 1917, p. 58.

Using Josh's entries above and below, create your own scenario as to what is happening with the relationship with Rena. (Remember to read between the lines, literally. In journals often some comment is added as ink could not be erased).

do not now for various reasons.

Saturday Mar. 10. To farm with Parley & father in morning then to Coalville to Principals meeting. Get haircut shave etc. Home 6:00 P.M. To practice at night Home 12:30 [Things look brighter.]

Sunday [illegible]

Journal, Saturday, March 10, 1917, p. 58.

Friday Mar. 16 To school until noon. Dismissed for Ward Reunion down to ward house and eat until I nearly burst. Home and get ready for dance and games at night. Referee one game. Stay to dance but do not have much of a time. Twisted things up a bit I suppose home 2:00.

Journal, Friday, March 16, 1917, p. 59

What do you think? Is Josh rough on himself? What would you do in his place?

Thursday Mar. 22 To school all day. Help R. wash dishes after school. Go to play meeting but we reach no conclusion as to what we are going to do. Have a rather peculiar talk after meeting. Come home and write poem, You do not care. I wonder why. To bed 1:30

Journal, Thursday, March 22, 1917, p. 60

Ah, Josh wrote a poem for Rena. What's the poem title? What is your prediction of Rena's reaction?

1917 =61=

Friday Mar 23 To school all day. Home down to hall over to store and school house. Call Rene in and read poem. I dont know what to think. Spend evening in playing singing reading and writing. Make application for Haytsville school for 1917-1918. Will hear from it in a few days I hope. To bed 9:45 I intend going after coal to morrow.

Journal, Friday, March 23, 1917, p. 61.

How was the poem received?

Josh wants a change in his life. What can he control right now?

Saturday Mar. 24. Up at 5:30 to Coalville after coal. There before the men are to work. Get a shave and start for home after getting X Floss shoed. Home and then back with Lid to Haytsville take R. down swallow something very hard But dont regret it So things turn out pretty good before this night is over. To bed 2:00

Journal, Friday, March 24, 1917, p. 61.

The Poem: Part Three—your thoughts:

Evidence is lacking - Yet I still hope.

April 2. Monday. Again I have a birthday twenty-two years old; a third of my life gone and not a great deal accomplished yet I'm trying to climb. To school all day. We had figured on going to Peoa to sing but it is very stormy and we back out. Home at night until R. comes over & take her home. Help wash dishes. Birthday present. To bed 11:15

Journal, Monday, April 2, 1917, p.64.

A third of his life over! What was the life expectancy of a man in 1917? How does Josh's compare?

What does this entry infer about his and Rena's relationship?

Life Expectancy Table

There is no evidence that this neck scarf is the present mentioned on his twenty-second birthday, but there is no other present from Rena mentioned in the journal and she did give him this scarf.

1917 =72=

I make some blunders

Evalville. I take Rena along.
Of course I make a perfect
ass of myself as usual. Back
by 10. Play and write in journal
study some and to bed about 10:30
May 2 To school all day. Up as far
Wednesday as Rockport to a dance
have a fairly good time

Journal, Tuesday & Wednesday, May 1-2, 1917, p. 72.

Thursday To school all day. We have
May 17. a small social at night R.
decides to go with me. Small
program and games and [illegible]
Still [illegible]

Journal, Thursday, May 17, 2017, p. 75.

Monday Up at 3:00 a.m. this morning
May 28. to take father and Mr Jorgensen
to Echo to catch 5:00 oclock train
Home sleep awhile afternoon
over to Smiths. Make a blunder

Journal, Monday, May 28, 1917, p. 77.

This appears to be a difficult courtship. How does Joshua feel each of these days?

Sunday June 3. To Sunday school in the morning meeting in the afternoon. Over to Smiths a while after church and again at night. Given a little information is it true or false?

Journal, Sunday June 3, 1917, p. 78.

Again, as I mentioned at the beginning of the chapter, young men of this era were such gentlemen that they were often too cryptic. Well, perhaps there were prying eyes of younger brothers to deal with also. What can you infer from this entry?

Friday June 15- Work up the canyon again with Bert. Home and get ready to go to Dance at Coalville alone. Get Haircut and sha

Journal, Friday June 15, 1917, p. 82.

What was different about this day?

a few. A night an old time dance here so we don't know where to go Oakley, Kamas or Park. We learn of a dance to Hoytsville so we go there & have an exceptionally good time, Misses Coddingtons are up. Home and abed 2:00

Journal, Wednesday, July 4, 1917, p. 87.

What did Josh do on this Independence Day?

Sunday July 15. Fay round home all day across the road toward evening have a cold reception of ice cream. Spend the evening with Miss Nelson.

Monday July 16. Work in hay all day for father. Over to see Miss Nelson at night another cold reception. Father goes to uncle Johns funeral

Tuesday July 17. Work in hay for father, all day. Home at night after singing practice.

Wednesday July 18. Work in hay all day, mend shoes in evening. Over to Smiths. Changes have taken place. Home 1:00

Journal, July 15-18, 1917, p. 89.

Who is receiving the "cold receptions?"

Who is giving the "cold receptions?"

Tuesday July 24. Wait at store for Everett to go up canyon and fix the car for his folks. I wait until 4:00 P.M. then I go up town eat supper and go to Saltair. He meets me out there afterward. See Rena, Dorus & Edith. Have a fairly good dance. Home on the last train. In bed 1:30.

Wednesday July 25. Up at noon. Get a shave and go up town for dinner. Have my picture taken. Up and get Rena up a Kirkes we go down town

Journal, Tuesday, July 24, 1917, p, 90.

What's different between Tuesday and Wednesday with his encounters with Rena?

Transcribe Wednesday's entry here:

Tuesday Aug 28 Work on Road over by Moores in fore-noon and for Lar Grow kin this afternoon. To dance with Rena at night a small crowd and poor time on account of certain things that came up. Home by 2:00

Wednesday Aug 29. Work for Lar Grow all day home take Rena Ride up canyon. Home supper music write in journal and to bed 10:00

Journal, Tuesday, August 28, 1917, p. 97.

What is the "tone" of Josh's writing voice? What is the evidence? Can you predict any outcomes for Josh and Rena?

Chapter 12: Josh the Poet

Mother.

Your princely halls and wealth untold.
Can never equal in pure gold,
The love of a mother for her son.
Measured not ~~by the~~ in pounds nor yet by Ton,
But By the acts of loving grace,
That makes to him his mothers face
Dearer fare than fame or power;
For to him she is the lofty tower
Of hope, of prayers, and love untold,
The one, who when young or growing old,
does loving acts of her own free will.
To ease our burdens or lift them, until
No matter how we love, father, sister, brother
None is so dear as our angle mother.

Use the next page to transcribe another sample of Joshua's writing. The first line has a few words that may be difficult to transcribe. Write out the letters you recognize, inserting an underscore to hold the places of mystery letters. Then say "goodbye" to the strange looking word and continue transcribing. Review the difficult words later after more experience with the page. Compare the words and the letters you did recognize with similar letters in the unknown word. Experiment with probable letters to see if inserting a letter creates an actual word that adds to the content.

Perfecting Detection Skills...Transcribe Joshua's Poem

Analysis of the Poem

1. Subject of the writing
2. The traits that Joshua shares about the subject
3. Joshua's feelings about the subject
4. Difficult words to transcribe (copy the words here, along with your transcription of the word).

Chapter 13: All in a Day's Work

This chapter divulges some of Josh's life as a teacher in 1916 and 1917. Use the spaces on the following pages provided for transcriptions or paraphrasing each excerpt.

riday Up in time to catch the morning
pr. 21 train to Coalville to give Eighth
Grade Examinations. Leave schoolbuilding
about 4:00 and go up to Mrs. Powell's
for supper. After Supper Parley &

Journal, Friday, April 21, 1916, p. 4.

turday Conduct Examinations in fore-noon,
ril 22. After dinner I help other principals
correct papers. Only one of my
Eighth grade Students got through.
To the show at night. To bed at Mrs.
Powells at 11:00

Journal, Saturday, April 22, 1916, p. 4.

Mon. April 24. To school all day. To show at night Walters Company presented "Sowing the Winds." A good play presented by a good cast of Characters. An English play of the upper class of society. Showing vice and corruptions of some of that class. To bed at 11:30.

Journal, Monday, April 24, 1916, p. 5.

Tuesday April 25. To school all day. To show at night Walters Company presented "Coriantor", by Orestus U. Bean: A Book of mormon play of rare quality. To bed at 11:15

Journal, Monday, April 25, 1916, p. 5.

Wednesday. May 10 To school all day. Down to meeting at night preparing for program at Homecoming of Oley Petersen.

Journal, Wednesday, May 10, 1916, p. 7.

Friday May 12 To school and checked up books and gave short program in forenoon. Gave the children a dance in the afternoon. Home and to-bed early.

Journal, Friday, May 12, 1916, p. 7.

Secretary desk built by Joshua, outside drawers were added by a cousin many years later.

May 24 We are going to plant potatoes in until 3:00. Then I come home and get ready to go to Coalville to the annual North Summit High School Banquet. Have a good time home and to-bed at 12-45.

Journal, Wednesday, May 24, 1916, p. 7.

Tuesday Sept 12 To school all day. Start Recitations to day Students as usual not very bright after a long rest. Home at night write three letters one to R. and to-bed 10:15

Journal, Tuesday, September 12, 1916, P. 30.

"New" Wanship School

North Summit High School, Coalville, Utah

Thursday Nov 16. To school all day. Have arithmetic nearly all day. The students are very dense or else I could not get it over to them.

Journal, Thursday, November 16, 1916, P. 41.

Sat. To school all day. To program
Dec 16 in Hall at night. School gives program.

Journal, Saturday, December 16, 1916, p. 45.

What does this photograph tell you about Joshua's working life?

- Appearance
- Dress
- Activity
- Extent of responsibilities

North Summit High School Basketball Coach

To childrens dance in afternoon and
get an invitation to dinner over to
Smiths. A good spread. We decide
to stay in Wanship for the Dance
at night if there is a good crowd but
if not we will leave for Coalville
after the Game of Basket Ball. A
fair crowd so we dance in Wanship.
Home at 9:45.

Journal, Monday, January 1, 1917, p. 49.

Friday Mar 23 To school all day. Home down to hill over to store and school house. Call Rena in and read poem. I don't know what to think. Spend evening in playing singing reading and writing. Make application for Haytsville school for 1917-1918. Will hear from it in a few days

Journal, Friday, March 23, 1917, p. 61.

Saturday April 7. To Coalville in morning on train to get a hair cut and see Mr. Neely about school teaching at Echo. Down to Sims with May Pinio in afternoon Eat supper at hotel. Call up R. and

Journal, Saturday, April 17, 1917, p. 65.

Grade book for the subject of ______________________.

What student name stands out? ________________________.

RECORD OF Geography CLASS FOR TERM ENDING........................TEACHER.

No.	NAMES.	1st Month.	2d Month.	3d Month.	4th Month.	5th Month.	Sum'ry.

Perfecting Detection Skills...Josh on Josh

Tuesday April 18. To School all Day. Talk of Wanship as a mining camp. Some good prospects. Wouldn't mind a millions myself. Correct papers at night and to bed

Journal, Tuesday, April 18, 1916, p. 3.

Saturday Aug 26. To Coalville after coal. Home at night. Write my journal to-bed by 10:00

Sunday Aug 27. Dress up and go down to go to Sunday School but back out. Home the largest part of the day. Up to Eld Young's in the afternoon we ride around some. At night we get Rena & Miss Cohn and go down the river for a ride. Home and to-bed by 12:00

Monday Aug 28. Work on foundation for garage. Haul gravel & mix cement. Home at night to-bed by 9:00

Journal, Tuesday, April 27 & 28, 1916, p. 25.

Saturday Dec 23. Up town and do some shopping. Back to Uncle Fred's and get supper. Everett works late so go up town myself on a little "rampage". Home 1:15

Journal, Saturday, December 23 1916, p. 47.

What I learned about Josh:

I wish I could see what I was good for and what would give me most happiness. Sometimes I'm tempted to take the bit in my teeth and forge ahead the next minute I want to lay down and stop trying. I wonder if I'm getting a square deal. I hope soon I will have some definate plans so I will have something to work to. I need an anchor. I can't find out what I want.

Journal, Tuesday, March 27, 1917, p. 62.

Wednesday April 4. To school all day. Over to Smiths a while after school. Home at night. Write letters and get journal up to date. Feel some like studying. I suppose I'll have to take charge of myself and give him a kick along occasionally.

Journal, Monday, April 4, 1917, p. 64.

Sun. April 22. To Sunday school and meeting. Preach in meeting on "True to Oneself." I don't know it impressed people. Home then over to Smith's

Journal, Sunday, April 22, 1917, p. 69.

Josh's writing about himself:

Something seems to be taking the best out of me & I can hardly imagine what it can be. I must pull myself together. I can't study as I should and don't get out of bed until 7.30 or 8.00 without a very great effort. I'm going to try for something better. My will power is not quite as strong as it was 6 months ago. I am going to get it back.

Friday April 27. To school all day. Get ready to go for Parley when he shows up and I get beat out of a trip. Home at night singing and playing. I think I'm getting myself better under control

Journal, April 26-27, 1917, p. 70.

What is the date of this entry?

What is the mood of his writing?

What could be happening in his life?

Adjectives to describe Josh based on all the entries?

More that you notice about Josh:

Thursday Aug 16. Take teachers examination all day. Uncle John Ann Nora Nita Mable and I go to Cabaret for the evening after a show. Have a good time

Friday Aug. 17 Teachers examination in forenoon afternoon spent at sheriffs office waiting for physical examination for military service. Leave for Wanship with Joe Clark about 4:30 P.M. Home and to dance at Hoytsville with Rena. Home 2:00

Sat. Aug. 18. Everett comes out with Earl. He and I go to Coalville for dinner. Ride & fool around together all day. Down to Hoytsville home and to Selby's to hear player piano. Cold night

Journal, August 16-17, 1917, p. 95.

How Accurate is Your Opinion of Yourself?

Write down what you see as your characteristics, and ask a few trusted friends to do the same on separate pieces of paper. Compile their answers. Then compare the lists.

My Characteristics: My List	My Characteristics: Friends' List

Chapter 15: War Comes to Josh

On a separate piece of paper, create a timeline to record all that relates to this chapter title. The first could read, " Sunday Feb 3, 1917: Reports of war with Germany." There may be multiple entries for one day. Just keep the dates in order, and summarize the major events. You can either download timeline templates, or draw your own; or you can just create a table.

Sunday Feb. 4. Rest all day. Reports of War with Germany. I hope they stay only reports and become nothing more. Rena comes over at night and talks quite awhile.

Journal, Sunday, February 3, 1917, p. 54.

On April 2, 1917, President Woodrow Wilson addressed Congress, asking for a declaration of war against Germany. Just over two months earlier, on January 31, the German government had announced its resumption of "unrestricted submarine warfare." With the announcement, German U-boats would without warning attempt to sink all ships traveling to or from British or French ports. Under the new strategy, U-boats had sunk three American merchant ships with a heavy loss of American life in March 1917. Two days after Wilson's speech, the Senate overwhelmingly declared that a state of war existed between Germany and the United States. Two days later the House of Representatives followed suit. The United States had entered "the Great War."

THE U.S. ARMY IN WORLD WAR I, 1917–1918, http://history.army.mil/books/amh-v2/PDF/Chapter01.pdf

April 2. Monday. Again I have a birthday twenty two years old; a third of my life gone and not a great deal accomplished yet I'm trying to climb. To school all day. We had figured on going to Roca to sing but it is very stormy and we back out. Home at night until R. comes over to take her home. Help wash dishes. Birthday present. To bed 11:15

Journal, Monday, April 2, 1917, p. 64.

Tuesday June 5. Up to farm in morning to clear away brush and work on the ditch until a little after-noon. Down and begin to get ready to go to Kamas to the dance. Registered today for military service. I suppose now the next thing will be a call to the front. To Kamas with Edd and Will at night. Sleep in Oakley. More evidence today. (Sincere Meeting)

Journal, Tuesday, June 5, 1917 p. 80.

Summit County Draft List

No. 1 Nick Peter.
No. 5 Fred Matson.
No. 6. Charles L. Peterson.
No. 10. Jefferson Ivie.
No. 15. J. E. Stine.
No. 17. Alfred Anderson.
No. 19. Peter Supar.
No. 23. Arvil Isaacson.
No. 25. George Clarence Payne.
No. 30. Archiball Cyrus Gehring.
No. 31. Robert I. Reynolds.
No. 36. James Cossey.
No. 43. Joseph Leon Robertson.
No. 46. Charles Autio.
No. 49. Herbert George Hewlett.
No. 52. George Harrison Hoover.
No. 56. Asa Clifton Neel.
No. 71 Hugh Johnson.
No. 75. Otho Clark Jenkins.
No. 90. Charles Edward Calvin.
No. 91. Ivan Meredith Cody.
No. 103. Andrew John Berg.
No. 107. Dean Storgis.
No. 112. Nick Rukavina.
No. 115. Ralph H. Townsend.
No. 122. John Mazar.
No. 124. Eugene Denton Sullivan.
No. 130. Manuel Fernandez.
No. 136. John Fors.
No. 140. Herbert Woodington.
No. 146. Arve Salonen.
No. 150. William McKenzie.
No. 154. Kenneth V. Decker.
No. 182. Leonard Stanford McPhee
No. 183. Lawrence C. Schaper.
No. 187. Fred Linderberg.
No. 191. Oscar Anderson.
No. 204. Willard J. Bircumshaw.
No. 222. Raymond Birnie.

(Continued from Page Two.)

No 156. Dominick Tassiner.
No. 164. Jakoy Zupan.
No. 168. Ray A. Thompson.
No. 169. John Johnson.
No. 593. George Gasparac.
No. 596. Fred E. Thomas.
No. 600. Frank A. Mcaughlin.
No. 601. David H. Gwilliams.
No. 604. Frank Towey.
No. 606. John L. Gibson.
No. 605. Jose Encinas.
No. 609. Rodger I. McDonough.
No. 613. Steves Wuskovich.
No. 617. James W. Sweatfield.
No. 620. John Stipich.
No. 622. Ernest Guard.
No. 623. Frank M. Burgener.
No. 627. Elwood Garvin.
No. 633. Bernard Fagan.
No. 635. Wm. Hyram Gordon.
No. 636. Morris Wight.
No. 637. Frank M. Stone.
No. 638. Charles I. Wilson.
No. 642. Drage Franich.
No. 645. Ace Davis.
No. 650. Ben Eccel.
No. 656. Newell Larson.
No. 664. John P. Houghton.
No. 675. Claued Fitch.
No. 677. Mike Geunith.
No. 705. Victor Andrew Neil.
No. 707. James Barry Pullar.
No. 713. John Penman.
No. 715. R. Holmbeck.
No. 721. Elmer Carlson.
No. 725. William John Neil.
No. 726. John Miller Johnson.
No. 735. Algot Erickson.
No. 738 Mike Kourlas.
No. 750. Peter Wuuckovich.
No. 755. William James Walsh.
No. 769. Uathan Kerr.
No. 772. George P. Gidley.
No. 775. Claude Archibald.
No. 776. Gus W. Sweatfield.
No. 778. John Ruotannen.
No. 783. Micheal John Mahay.
No. 784. Henry Tikkeman.
No. 800. Matt Brklacch.
No. 805. John Rukavan.
No. 806. Tony Rukavan.
No. 808. FFrank Tomlonovich.
No. 809. Daniel Hyram Bates.
No. 814. George Moore.
No. 822. Albert Conce Dray.
No. 832. John Sullivan.
No. 837. Marion Linich.

No. 356—Charles Henry Moore.
No. 357—Juan Antonio Montoga.
No. 421—George Kokiananos.
No. 430Nick Louridos.
No. 542—Ross Rigby.
No. 574—Karto Roezoff.
No. 619—Jose Lopez.
No. 741—Christ Biozos.
No. 802—Naum Patroff.
No. 829—James Saderakos.
No. 841—Grindna Meabo.
No. 856—Benjamin C. Dye. ......
No. 895—Frank Lester Dall.
No. 948—Vervave Gutiere.
No. 982—Earl Phin McDonald.

ECHO.
No. 205—Cust Zarokastas.
No. 513—Alfred Marlow Jones.
No. 652—Luther Moody Perry.
No. 744—George Dewling.
No. 872—Jim Choocatos.
No. 933—Nignel Roaha.
No. 949—Hyrum F. Keelow.
No. 1004—Norman Earl Brewer.

UPTON.
No. 18—George Warburton.
No. 673—George Apollice Gamble.
No. 692—Charles Stringfellow.
No. 704—Joseph Elmer Blonquist.

OAKLEY.
No. 206—Ardlebert Miles.
No. 229—Thomas Ralph Wilde.
No. 436—Byron Dean Stevens.
No. 511—Frank Johnson.
No. 576—Douglas W. Reeve.
No. 749—Clarence Ray Frazier.
No. 926—Ruben Leonard Frazier.
No. 927—David Hartwell Welsh.

WOODLAND.
No. 76—Thomas Urwin.
No. .432—Paul Ernest Knight.

ROCKPORT.
No. 117—Alonlo Salisbury.
No. 168—Harold CCossey.
No. 810—Albert Cossey.
No. 972—Andres F. Larson.
No. 1008—Francis Osker Farnon.

BLACK FORK CAMP.
No. 54—Gustof H. Samuelson.
No. 121—Valdemar A. Mytrenke.
No. 202—Jos Tomich.
No. 320—Leragan Bardizabian.
No. 327—Elmer Johnson.
No. 328—Arthur Daniels.
No. 456—Joan Gustol Anderson.
No. 736—Otto F. W. Nelson.
No. 861—Johanes Johnson.
No. 911—Peter H. E. Holmberg.

(Continued on next page)

No. 204. Willard J. Bircumshaw.
No. 222. Raymond Birnie.
No. 228. Lewis W. Strongman.
No. 240. John Bur.
No. 257. Robert Birnie.
No. 258. Harry L. Nuckolls.
No. 265. Lawrence J. Workman.
No. 269. Erick Joffs.
No. 272. Guy Lawrence Swanson.
No. 274. Henry Zoret.
No. 280. Charles Holm.
No. 284. Leander Mattson Wils.
No. 285. Vern Leroy Holiday.
No. 292. Winslou Lora.
No. 298. Alex Hugh McDonald.
No. 299. John Edward McLeod.
No. 305. Victor Ladevich.
No. 307. George Thorp.
No. 309. John Dobniker.
No. 310. Wolfgang Simeth.
No. 311. Paulo Satta.
No. 316. Joe Buklacich.
No. 321. Eino Takala.
No. 325. Emil Bloomquist.
No. 331. Herman F. Andrew.
No. 332. Alfred Sundquist.
No. 341. Gust Carlson.
No. 342. Andrew Sandstrom.
No. 343. Uno Sudquist.
No. 344. Carl Hove.
No. 346. Henry Hanks.
No. 349. Satuinino Valenzulea.
No. 350. Howard Breen.
No. 352. Edward Anderly.
No. 353. William Lowry.
No. 356. Edward F. Hamilton.
No. 363. Hugo Hakanson.
No. 379. Theo Johnson, Jr.
No. 388. Herbert Kneebone.
No. 390. Henry R. Kramer.
No. 392. Mike Caros.
No. 393. Sterling S. Lewis.
No. 396. Jacob Held, Jr.
No. 406. Douglas Cameron McKay.
No. 410. Pete Giovota.
No. 418. Joseph E. Weeter.
No. 422. John Hanley.
No. 427. Kirtlang P. Girard.
No. 433. Ben Madurich.
No. 435. William Miller.
No. 437. William J. Chivrell.
No. 438. Andrew W. Johnson.
No. 440. John Gilbert.
No. 447. George William Wilde.
No. 452. John Bubbas.
No. 486. Robert L. McLaren.
No. 487. John Barber.
No. 492. Leland Dale Mortenson.
No. 499. Martin Axel Carlson.
No. 501. Moris V. Andra, Jr.
No. 504. Matt Rodolack.
No. 514. Harry Bush.
No. 524. Nick Budovich.
No. 525. Ray Gibbons.
No. 526. Ray Pace.
No. 530. George Kummer.
No. 536. Henry T. Hobson.
No. 543. Nck Skelin.
No. 544. George Spiron.
No. 546. Leo Daniels.
No. 550. Tim Shea.
No. 552. Percy S. Aubrey.
No. 555. Robert Dunbar.
No. 556. Nickels Hiristtopulos.
No. 562. Shirley C. McBride.
No. 565. William Murphy.
No. 566. James F. Shanley.
No. 567. Oscar Poerson.
No. 582. Mike Silovitch.
No. 588. Joseph C. Schoney.

Continued on Page Seven

No. [illegible]. Albert Conce Dray.
No. 832. John Sullivan.
No. 837. Marion Linich.
No. 838. Fred Mortinson.
No. 848. Michael C. O'Conner.
No. 857. James Murphy.
No. 862. Leland Williams.
No. 866. Walace Williams.
No. 867. John Bukavitch.
No. 868. Harold McKinnon.
No. 871. E. D. Berk.
No. 874. Frank Collma.
No. 877. John Chambers.
No. 880. Herman R. Rundle.
No. 882. James W. Jacobs.
No. 886. Newton Tittle Smith.
No. 889. Gust A. Anderson.
No. 896. Lemuel Peter Sweeney.
No. 900. James Peter Panterizrs.
No. 906. Orville W. Lefler.
No. 919. Arthur Rowe.
No. 920. Angelos Chilos.
No. 924. Victor Sandstrom.
No. 929. Dolphie R. Sessions.
No. 930. Edwin Garhard Orsten.
No. 935. Edward Jouve.
No. 939. Lewis Malin.
No. 940. James N. Neil.
No. 944. George Salinovch.
No. 946. William Frausa.
No. 950. Max E. Sullivan.
No. 957. Erick Strom.
No. 961. Isaac Homake.
No. 965. Joseph Bamonte.
No. 966. William E. Shea.
No. 968. John F. Campbell.
No. 974. Oto Roeseler.
No. 978. Henry Nyfars.
No. 983. Patrick J. Quinn.
No. 985. Joseph John Walker.
No. 989. Clyde Andrew Peterson.
No. 993. Arthur L. Peterson.
No. 1002. Pontelin Garsia.
No. 1010. Henry Kenneth Gibson.
No. 1014. Dong Wing Joe.
No. 1016. Alfrado Calalloro.
No. 1021. Wm. Rolfe, Jr.
No. 1023. George E. Arty.
No. 1028. John Dafais.
No. 1031. Clarence G. Gates.
No. 1032. Jacob Buscia.
No. 1034. Mike Siliga.
No. 1035. Tony Stipich.
No. 1043. Paul Avery Downer.
No. 1046. Joseph Gasgarac.
No. 1048. Ray John Farrell.
No. 1050. Wm. Alexander Wortley.
No. 1057. Vern Blanquist.
No. 1058. Hugh Henderson.
No. 1059. Jacob A. Schuster.
No. 1064. Joseph Hammerlund.
No. 1067. LaPage H. Raddon.
No. 1070. Fred Koet.
No. 1073. Ray Stevens.

Those drafted outside of Park City:

HENEFER.
No. 2 John G. Anderson.
No. 278 Samuel A. Bunot.
No. 368—Joseph Johnson.
No. 400—Neil P. Lythgoe.
No. 506—Orson S. Dawson.
No. 548—Horace Hillman Richins.
No. 549—Fred O'Brien.
No. 557—Ernest Herbert Brewer.
No. 560—Washington O. Stevens.
No. 563—Joel L. Boatright.
No. 564—John Alma Bunot.
No. 676—Heber Dearden.
No. 747—Edward P. Pasket.
No. 766—John Hyrum Frances.
No. 854—Warfen John Richins.
No. 963—Oscar Elmer Dawson.
No. 981—Ephrain Taylor.

KAMAS.
No. 8—Bernard Gould Williams.
No. 11—Bernard Edward Evans.
No. 61—Raymond L. Knight.
No. 86—Oscar Walker Royce.
No. 186—Leonard Marino.
No. 212—Walter Melvin Jones.
No. 287—Clifford Warr.
No. 391—Roy Grant Lambert.
No. 420—R[illegible]ard F. Lambert, Jr.
No. 444—William Woolstenhulme.
No. 585—Lawrence W. Prescott.
No. 624—Jesse P. O'Driscoll.
No. 700—Merit W. Pack, Jr.
No. 714—Lester Edward Osborne.
No. 824—Hugh Henry Erekson.
No. 879—Nathan Harwood White.
No. 905—George Leo Wilde.
No. 1022—Mont C. Carpenter.

CASTLE ROCK.
No. 93—Pancho Auenasoff.
No. 113—James Mazarakos.
No. 199—William Thomas Nichols.
No. 211—Dimitar I. Chochoff.
No. 271—Kasrof S. Hakigian.
No. 303—Daniel Reed Miller.
No. 323—Athanasios Daskalopouls.

No. 736—Otto F. W. Nelson.
No. 861—Johanes Johnson.
No. 911—Peter H. E. Holmberg.
No. 979—Tuffil Revore.

EMORY.
No. 58—Anton V. Morkoff.
No. 336—Bawdon Bodosian.
No. 442—Frank Blaine Devine.
No. 781—Salm Kasparian.
No. 913—Simon Hartenian.

COALVILLE.
No. 72—George Daniel Keaton.
No. 86—George Ernest Willough.
No. 133—Curtis Anton Lamb.
No. 268—Ralph Carr Wright.
No. 297—Frank Steart Allen.
No. 312—Franklin R. Salmon.
No. 335—William Henry Arnold.
No. 337—William R. Birch.
No. 378—Clarence Reuben Wilde.
No. 441—Duncan Angus Maxwell.
No. 450—Bayard C. Taylor.
No. 481—Ray Morbay.
No. 509—William Earl Calderwood
No. 602—Samuel Wright.
No. 679—James Walton.
No. 760—Samuel Smith.
No. 773—Harvey W. Robinson.
No. 792—William Egbest Saxton.
No. 836—William Joseph Wilde.
No. 840—Jacob C. Blonqdst.
No. 843—William H. Branch, Jr.

FRANCIS.
No. 102—James L. Atkinson.
No. 105—Amos Clive Atkinson.
No. 571—Thomas Ashael Prescot.
No. 590—Benjamin Page.
No. 691—Heber M. Prescott.
No. 797—Milton John Richardson.
No. 1011—Heber March McNeil.

HOYTSVILLE.
No. 126—William R. Sargent.
No. 132—Robert Steven Hiller.
No. 175—Winifred Walter West.
No. 223—James Byron Birch.
No. 275—George Earl Wilkinson.
No. 407—William Everett Gunn.
No. 424—Wilford Nephi Sargent.
No. 770—David Leroy Sargent.
No. 851—Richard Oscar Birch.
No. 883—Byron Winters.

GRASS CREEK.
No. 94—Joseph Leroy Wilde.
No. 369—James Lee Gillespie.

MILL CREEK CAMP.
No. 267—Sam Johnsen.
No. 462—Pete Moudy Gardine.
No. 493—Axoil Edwin Sellig.
No. 519—Jack Oja.
No. 657—Erik John Neilson.
No. 860—George Edward Bowen.
No. 934—John Ljolund.
No. 964—Reuben Isaarson.
No. 970—Clus Tyko Issarson.
No. 1065—Bros. T. Tanglund.

PEOA.
No. 123—Jerold S. Bleazard.
No. 372—Hyrum Willis Jorpenson.
No. 383—Gorden Frankling Wright
No. 477—Oscar Franklin Jansen.
No. 634—Stephen Casper Marchant
No. 739—Ammon Seth Wright.
No. 757—Thomas Earl Neel.
No. 786—Walter Ole Wright.
No. 928—John Reuben Marchant.

WANSHIP.
No. 470—Jospua Henry Bates.
No. 488—Albert Thomas Smith.
No. 616—Willard John Gibbons.
No. 699—Albert Moore Gibbons.
No. 1007—Edwin Russell Young.

MARION.
No. 212—Lawrence Larsen.
No. 458—Mark Harper Peterson.
No. 507—Earl Davis.
No. 581—George Delmer Simpson.
No. 631—William H. Lemon.
No. 707—James Barry—Amonte, Ontario, Canada.

PARLEYS PARK.
No. 711—Victor E. Peterson.
No. 1066—George Lucins Felton.

Park Record, July 7, 1917. p. 2 , 7 . Utah Digital Newspapers. http://udn.utah.edu/cdm/ref/collection/park2/

REGISTRATION CARD No. 9

1	Name in full: Joshua Henry Bates (Given name) (Family name)	Age in yrs. 22
2	Home address: Wanship Summit Co. Utah (State)	
3	Date of birth: April 2 1895 (Month) (Day) (Year)	
4	Are you (1) a natural-born citizen, (2) a naturalized citizen, (3) an alien, (4) or have you declared your intention (specify which)? Natural Born	
5	Where were you born? Wanship Utah U.S.A. (Town) (State) (Nation)	
6	If not a citizen, of what country are you a citizen or subject? —	
7	What is your present trade, occupation, or office? Farming A!	
8	By whom employed? Joshua Bates Where employed? Wanship	
9	Have you a father, mother, wife, child under 12, or a sister or brother under 12, solely dependent on you for support (specify which)? None	
10	Married or single (which)? Single Race (specify which)? Caucasion	
11	What military service have you had? Rank None; branch — years —; Nation or State —	
12	Do you claim exemption from draft (specify grounds)? None	

I affirm that I have verified above answers and that they are true.

Joshua Henry Bates (Signature or mark)

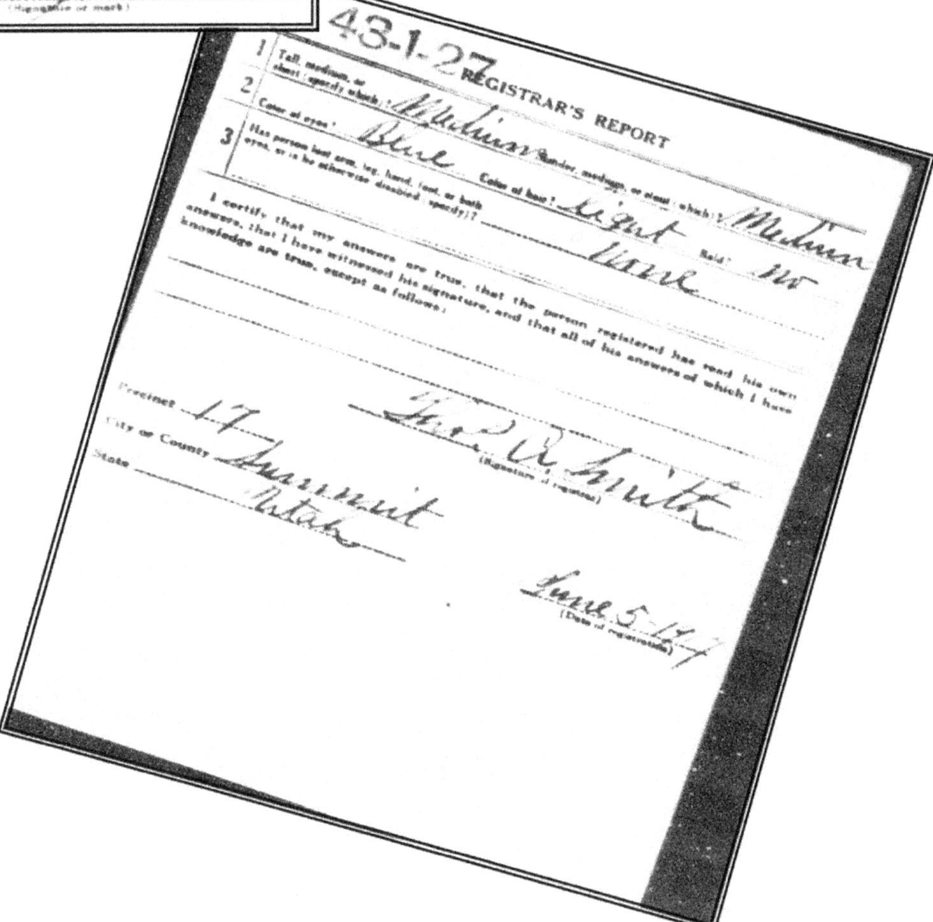

43-1-27

REGISTRAR'S REPORT

1. Tall, medium, or short (specify which)? Medium Slender, medium, or stout (which)? Medium
2. Color of eyes? Blue Color of hair? Light Bald? No
3. Has person lost arm, leg, hand, foot, or both eyes, or is he otherwise disabled (specify)? None

I certify that my answers are true, that the person registered has read his own answers, that I have witnessed his signature, and that all of his answers of which I have knowledge are true, except as follows:

Geo. A. Smith (Signature of registrar)

Precinct 17
City or County Summit
State Utah

June 5-1917 (Date of registration)

United States, Selective Service System. *World War I Selective Service System Draft Registration Cards, 1917-1918*. Washington, D.C.: National Archives and Records Administration. M1509, 4,582 rolls. Imaged from Family History Library microfilm.

Tuesday July 3. Wrote for Mr Smith all day. Rode to Park City with Charlie Hertz at night to help do same work on Registration cards. Slept at hotel.

Journal, Thursday, July 3, 1917, p. 86.

Blogs |

Search Archives

Research Our Records | Veterans Service Records | Teachers' Resources | Our Locations

Military Records

Home > Research Our Records > Military Records > WWI > Draft Registration > World War I Draft Registration Cards: Utah

Research Our Records

Main Page
What's New?
New Accessions
On Our Partners' Web Sites
Get Started

World War I Draft Registration Cards Microfilm Roll List, M1509: Utah (19 rolls)

Roll	Description	Surname
UT1	Be...	
	Bo...	

	Sevier County	A-Z
	Summit County	A-L
UT16	Summit County	Mc-Z
	Tooele County	A-Z

The *FamilySearch* description of the United States World War I draft registration cards. The Federal government had to register men, as only about 80,000 volunteered. The government hoped for 1 million.

FamilySearch | Family Tree | Memories | Search | Indexing | Sign In | Free Account

RECORDS | GENEALOGIES | CATALOG | BOOKS | WIKI

United States World War I Draft Registration Cards, 1917-1918

Description

Name index and images of draft registration cards for World War I. Three registrations occurred between 1917 and 1918. The 1st was held 5 Jun 1917 for men ages 21-31. The 2nd was held 5 Jun 1918 for men who turned 21 since the 1st registration. The 3rd started 12 Sep 1918 for men ages 18-45. The collection includes cards for 24 million men. The cards are arranged by state, by city or county, by local draft board, then alphabetical by surname. While images for all draft cards are available in the browse the index is 96% complete. The index is not yet complete for Illinois, Indiana, Michigan, Nebraska, Nevada, Ohio, Puerto Rico, Utah, Washington, and Wisconsin. The draft registration cards are part of Record Group 163, Records of the Selective Service System (WWI), 1917-1939, and is National Archives Microfilm publication M1509.

Thursday July 26 Up late out to uncle Freds for dinner. Clara and I go up town get mother a hat then we look at the proofs of my picture I order a dozen. Start home with Clara but go back to telephone to Floss. I make a date for Friday. Everett and I go up town to a show then play Pool until 11:45

Friday July 27 Out to uncle Freds. get clothes pressed and go up town. Catch the 11:15 electric train for Springville there by 1:00. Floss meets me at the ~~tra~~ station takes me to their home and have dinner. Around town a little in afternoon. Over to Spanish Fork to an excelant dance at night.

Journal, July 26-27, 1917, p. 91.

Remember this studio photograph from Chapter One? Now you can record the date Josh looked at his photo proofs.

____

Why a photograph now?

Find Joshua's reference to his physical examination on the next page and circle it.

Date of this letter:

____

Date of the exam:

____

PARK CITY, UTAH AUG 14 7-AM 1917

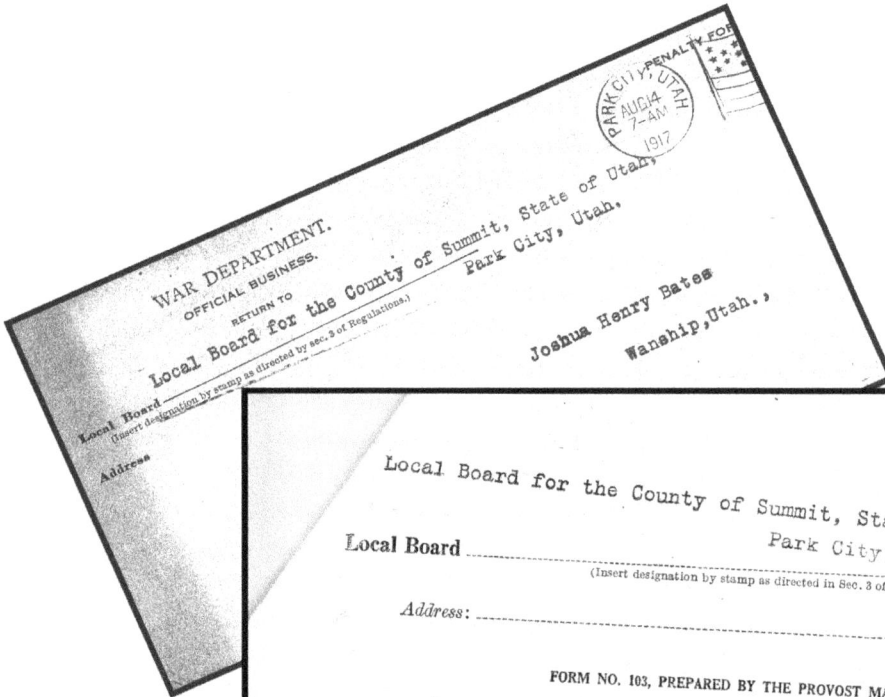

PENALTY FOR

WAR DEPARTMENT.

OFFICIAL BUSINESS.

RETURN TO

Local Board for the County of Summit, State of Utah, Park City, Utah.

Local Board (Insert designation by stamp as directed by sec. 3 of Regulations.)

Address

Joshua Henry Bates

Wanship, Utah.,

Local Board for the County of Summit, State of Utah, Park City, Utah. **Serial No.** 470

Local Board (Insert designation by stamp as directed in Sec. 3 of Regulations.)

Address:

FORM NO. 103, PREPARED BY THE PROVOST MARSHAL GENERAL.

NOTICE OF CALL AND TO APPEAR FOR PHYSICAL EXAMINATION.

To Joshua Henry Bates (Name.)

Wanship, Utah., (Address on registration card.)

You are hereby notified that pursuant to the act of Congress approved May 18, 1917, you are called for military service of the United States by this Local Board from among those persons whose registration cards are within the jurisdiction of this Local Board.

Your Serial Number is 470, and your Order Number is 200

You will report at the office of this Local Board for physical examination on the 17th (Day.) day of August (Month.), 1917 (Year.), at 1 o'clock P. M.

Any claim for exemption or discharge must be made on forms which may be procured at the office of this Local Board, and must be filed at the office of this Local Board on or before the SEVENTH day after the date of mailing this notice.*

Your attention is called to the penalties for violation or evasion of the Selective Service law, approved May 18, 1917, and of the Rules and Regulations made pursuant thereto, which penalties are printed on the back hereof.

LOCAL BOARD For Summit County, Utah.,

By P. H. Ryan *Chairman.*

A. C. Hoskin *Clerk.*

* Date of mailing notice, 13th (Day.) of August (Month.), 1917 (Year.)

63—4474

night.

Thursday Aug 16. Take teachers examination all day. Uncle John Ann Nora Nita Mable and I go to Cabaret for the evening after a show. Have a good time

Friday Aug. 17 Teachers examination in forenoon afternoon spent at sheriffs office waiting for physical examination for military service. Leave for Wanship with Joe Clark about 4:30 P.M. Home and to dance at Hoytsville with Anna. Home 2:00

Sat. Aug. 18. Everett comes out with Earl. He and I go to Coalville for dinner. Ride & fool around together all day. Down to Hoytsville home and to Selby's to hear player piano. Cold night

Journal, Aug 16-18, 1917, p. 95.

the morning.

Thursday Aug 23 Up at 5:00 to start for home. Stop in Willard to get some fruit. Lunch at Five Points. Get fruit at Uinta. Home 7:15. To Farewell party for Roy Haner at night. He has enlisted for the marines. Home 1:30

Journal, Thursday, August 23, 1917, p. 96.

Don't start reading yet!

Just hold the page back and look for anomalies in Josh's writing style, how it appears on the page. Circle the part. Now you may read and decide what is going on.

=100=

Tuesday Sept. 11 To school all day. Home and Read at night. To bed early

Wednesday Sept. 12 School all day play Pool and write letters bed 11:30.

Thursday Sept. 13. To school all day. Read the Two Vanrevels. By Booth Tarkington. To bed 11:00

Friday Sept 14. To school all day. Home to Holt 3:30. Get ready for Parley to come after me after shaving. Sit around until 8:45 to dance at Coalville with Rena Home 1:00

Saturday Sept. 15. Up 8:00 down to Post Office and get call to report for military duty Wednesday. Work on car After dinner go to Coalville. Hair cut shave etc the business and on to Echo for my clothes and books back to Coalville up to Glenn's to Drug store home. 10:30. to bed 11:45.

Sunday Sept. 16. Do not go to sunday school. Or meeting Parley and I leave for Roy 3:00 P.M. Do not get to see Vera to-night go over to uncle Toms. To bed 12:30

Mon. Sept. 17. Up early to prepare to start have leave 8:30 Stop along for fruit Home 3:00 Over to Smiths in afternoon. Take Rena to Farewell party at night. We have

Journal, September 11-17 1917, p. 100.

= 101 =

a good time. Bert & I make a
little speech. Home 1.30 A.M.

Tue. Sept 18 Work in field same to-day write
letters. Home in early part of evening
Over to Smiths at night. Home 12.00

Wednesday Sept. 19 To day I leave to put myself
under military service. I shall
no doubt find myself in a
new experience The folks ~~seem~~
~~to~~ take my leaving quite hard.
It makes it harder for me but
I must face up! Will try and
continue my journal. We leave
Utah Tomorrow

Journal, September 18-19, 1917, p. 101.

Transcribe Wednesday, September 19, 1917 here:

A Farewell to Soldier Boys

Agreeing with The Record that proper recognition was not being given the boys who are called to serve their country, Mr. C. C. Nichols and Miss Dena Thompson, interested themselves in getting up a grand farewell ball, that our citizens might meet the boys and wish them god speed on their patriotic mission.

This lady and gentleman have met with gratifying success, and next Monday night a grand ball will be given at Rasband's Hall, to which every soldier boy is cordially invited, and every patriotic citizen urged to attend to give cheer and praise to the departing heros.

A pleasinp feature of this demonstration is the fact that Mr. Rasband has donated his hall for the occasion, the Park City Independent Band has volunteered to furnish the music free of charge, and everything in connection with the affair will be given free of cost to the lady and gentleman, who are responsible for the event.

A charge of one dollar per couple will be made, and every cent received for tickets will be given to the boys selected from this county to fight for their flag and country.

It should be a great event and the hall filled to overflowing.

The ladies who are assisting in details for the farewell, in decorating the hall, etc., are Miss Eleanor Wright, Miss Mary Gwilliams, Miss Amber Stanley, Miss Emma Thompson, Mish Grace Thomphon and Miss Ethel Hales.

It must be remembered that this is not a local affair so far as the soldier boys are concerned, but every drafted man in the county is urged to attend the dance as guests—it is only those who escaped the draft who are asked to buy a ticket.

Got enthused and make the big farewell ball a pleasing, patriotic success.

THE SECOND CALL.

Following are the names of those selected for the second call of 40 per cent of Summit county's draft. These boys will leave Park City next Thursday morning, for Camp Lewis, American Lake, Washington:

Heber L. Dearden, Dean Sturgis, Hyrum Willis Jorgensen, Victor, Sandstrom, Paul Ernest Knight, Ammon Seth Wright, Henry R. Kramer, Walter Ole Wright, Andres Ferdnand Larsen, William E. Shea, Harold J. McKinnon, Frank Collins, Percy Aubrey, John Miller Johnson, Roy Gibbons Howard Breen, Frank Monroe Burgner, Eric Joffs, Edwin Russel Young, William Lawry, Frank Marion Stone, Albert Thomas Smith, Harry Hanks, Raymon Leo Knight, Douglas Cameron McKay, George Clarence Payne, Gustof Albert Anderson, Raymond Birnie, Orvil William Lefler, Otto Rosseler, Arthur Rowe, Joseph Hammerlund, Joshua Henry Bates, George Edwin Addy, Wilford Nephi Sargent, James Murphy, Herman Rosel Rundille, William Murphy, Hyrum Cossey, Shirley Curtis McBride, William Miller, William John Neil, Norman Carl Brewer, Robert Birnie, Klyde Andrew Peterson, Thomas Ralph Wilde, Lewis W. Strongman, Ralph Parke, Robert Heber Hiller, Carl Hove, William Hyrum Gorden.

What can be included in the timeline?

1. Why was the grand farewell ball given?
2. What was done with the entry fees to the ball?
3. What is the date of this news article?
4. When are the "soldier boys" to leave for Camp Lewis according to this article?
4. Compare this with Joshua's journal entries. What do you notice?

Good-Bye, God Speed, Safe Return!

Notwithstanding the lack of interest and apparent indifference at the departure of Park City's first assignment of soldier boys for faraway camps, the real loyal and patriotic spirit of our citizens were manifested yesterday morning when the fifty-one of the flower of Summit county's manhood left for training quarters at Camp Lewis, Washington.

The first feature that stirred the patriotism of early risers was the sounding of reveille by Willard Bircumshaw from the porch of his home on Rossie Hill.

Then came Leader Zack Oblad of the Park City Military Band, with as many members of his band that he was able to get together, and patriotic airs were played—bringing pride and at the same time real sadness and heartaches, because of the going away of sons, husbands and sweethearts.

Before 6:30 a. m. all the soldier boys were at the Union Pacific station, together with hundreds of citizens to grasp their hands, to say good bye, and to wish them godspeed and a safe return home to mother, to wife, to sister and other loved ones.

As the hour for the train to depart drew near, greater became the assemblage, and heart-rending indeed was the scene of fond farewells, of lingering, loving kisses, of tearful eyes, fervent embraces and prayful "God Bless You."

The large majority of the departing ones were tear stained and sorrowful, while some were jolly—the latter dong much to dispel the gloom that overhung the crowd.

The train left the station at 7:05 amid cheers and hat waving and final good byes shouted by hundreds of friends and loved ones.

It was a magnificent demonstration—one long to be remembered by the departing ones as well as those "left behind."

The boys were comfortably provided for in a Pullman tourist, and will go direct to Camp Lewis, Washington, the contingent being in charge of Douglas C. McKay.

Frank Marion Stone, whose name was published last week, and who should have left with the rest, was given until October 5th, for further investigation into his claim for exemption, and Frank Shanley was substituted in his stead. For the benefit of our readers we re-publish the names of those who made up the second call:

Heber L. Deardon, Dean Sturgis, Hyrum Willis Jorgenson, Victor Sandstrom, Paul Ernest Knight, Ammon Seth Wright, Henry R. Kramer, Walter Ole Wright, Andres Ferdnand Larsen, William E. Shea, Harold J. McKinnon, Frank Collins, Percy Aubrey, John Miller Johnston, Roy Gibbons, Howard Breen, Frank Monroe Burgner, Eric Joffs, Edwin Russel Young, William Lawry, Frank Shanley, Albert Thomas Smith, Harry Hanks, Raymon Leo Knight, Douglas Cameron McKay, George Clarence Payne, Gustof Albert Anderson, Raymond Birnie, Orvil William Lefler, Otto Rosseler, Arthur Rowe, Joseph Hammerlund, Joshua Henry Bates, George Edwin Addy, Wilford Nephi Sargent, James Murphy, Herman Rosel Rundille, William Murphy, Hyrum Cossey, Shirley Curtis McBride, William Miller, William John Neil, Norman Carl Brewer, Robert Birnie, Klyde Andrew Peterson, Thomas Ralph Wilde, Lewis W. Strongman, Ralph Parke, Robert Heber Hiller ,Carl Hove, William Hyrum Gorden.

THE SOLDIER'S FAREWELL.

Thanks to the efforts of Miss Dena Thompson and Mr. C. C. Nichols, and the young ladies named by them to assist in the Farewell Ball in honor of the soldier boys called into service, was a grand success, Rasband's hall being filled with as fine and jolly a crowd as ever gathered in a ball room.

The hall was beautifully decorated with flags and bunting, with appropriate placards here and there displayed, clever handiwork of Mr. R. K. Thomas, of the Welsh, Driscoll & Buck establishment.

A committee of young ladies were in the receiving line, and every 'soldier boy' was distinguished by the pinning on of a small American flag.

Rev. P. A. Simpkins, of Salt Lake, was present for a few minutes, and gave one of his characteristic talks, complimenting those who thus honored the brave men who were about to leave home to enter the service of Uncle Sam, and giving words of cheer and praise to the guests of honor, briefly telling what the war meant, and admonishing them to do their full duty—and when occasion required to "shoot straight."

The distinguished visitor was enthusiastically applauded—and made friends and admirers, as he always does.

Later in the evening Mr. Welsh, on behalf of those in whose honor the ball wah given, thanked those who were responsible for the splendid event.

The receipts from the ball netted the "tobacco fund," $212.00, giving to each Park City boy now enrolled $4.00. Good indeed.

The music by the Park City Independent Band, whose services were donated was the best ever, and won unstinted praise from the dancers.

EXPRESSIONS OF THANKS.

Miss Thompson and Mr. Nichols desire to publicly thank the following named for donations responsible for the big financial success: The Park City Military Band, Welsh, Driscoll & Buck, Mrs. Wm. Kneale, The Park Record, J. J. Fitzgerald, R. K. Thomas, Jim Don and 'Bill' Collins.

PARK BOYS ENLIST.

The departing of the soldiers boys Thursday morning was too much for three of our home boys, and they decided when the good byes and god speeds were over to go forth and fight for their country with the rest of the sterling youths of the country. These young men, James Grisley, Sterl Marchant and Joe Holland, all having good jobs at the King Coalition, drew their time yesterday morning, and left Park City on the afternoon stage for Salt Lake where they will enlist in the navy—if they pass physical examination, which they are sure to do.

And thus the flower of American manhood is becoming involved in this great world's struggle, and the hearts of proud parents torn with fear and anxiety for their boys.

The action of the three young men mentioned above is indeed patriotic, and bespeaks for them the trueAmerican spirit.

May they win laurels in the service of their country and return to their homes is the wish of every Parkite.

Park Record, September 9, 1917, *Utah Digital Newspapers, http://udn.lib.utah.edu/digital/unews*

Events reported in this article for the timeline:

Joshua H. Bates
Cor. D #347 M.G. Bn.
Indintification number
2,255,462
Two million, two hundred and
fifty-five thousand, four hundred
and sixty two.

Transcribe here:

The call to duty Join the Army for home and country. (n.d.). Retrieved April 27, 2016, from http://www.loc.gov/pictures/item/00651808/

GUARANTEE TO THE PUBLIC

IDENTIFICATION
OF THE OWNER OF THIS BOOK

Name Joshua H. Bates
Business Address
Residence Address Wanship, Utah
Birthday
Telephone Number, Office

Journal of J. H. Bates
Wanship, Utah.
Sept. 19. 1917 Wed.
Report at Sheriffs office for military service We are told, that we must be ready to take the train at Park city at 6:00 A.M. Back to Wanship. To party at night. Presents given me were Pen from Parley Watch from father & mother and a ring from the people of the town.
Thur. Sept. 20, 1917
Up all night. Leave for Park City with Bert, Ed and Led at 4:30, Break fast and take train

Josh started his military diary in a small pocket journal he picked up at a tailoring store in Salt Lake City. It is only 4 3/4 by 2 3/4 inches, quite a difference from the notebook-sized journal of the last two years.

Transcribe the first page.

Perfecting Comprehension Skills...Journal, Photographs, Postcards, Letters and Telegrams

Large crowd bids farewell
at Park. When we reached
Wanship the whole town was
out to greet us and we
certainly felt well about
it. Good-bys over we traveled
to Coalville where we
were greeted again. We
spent about 5 hrs in Echo. While
there I visited school. Mother
Mrs Smith, Mrs Horner &
Stella and Rena came down.
Leave Ogden after 2 hrs.
wait there. Sleep until
we are well into Idaho.
Friday Sept 21 1917
Travel all day through
Idaho going north

To bed. 8:30 Sleep soundly
Saturday Sept 22 1917.
Travel stop awhile at
Portland Ore then on north
to Washington. Land at
Camp Lewis about 12:30 PM.
Pass through Doctors tent
then on to quarters.
Dinner. Drill. Lecture
at night. To bed 8:30
[illegible] Damp cold weather
have not seen sun.
Sunday Sept. 23, 1917
Up at 5:30. Around
quarters in morning.
Over to lake in Afternoon.
Write letters to Red.

Answer the questions on the next page about these entries.

Page 2:

1. List the Utah towns the train traveled through after he left Wanship.

2. Who came to wish him farewell?

3. What state after Utah did the train cross?

Page 3:

1. In what state is Portland?

2. List all that the draftees did once they arrived at Camp Lewis.

3. What does Josh complain about?

"*Camp Lewis* was the first military installation in the history of our nation to be created as the direct result of an outright gift of land by citizens themselves."

Since 1902 local and state leaders had advocated a Northwest location. Germany's submarine attacks increased and the United States had entered the war before the 70,000 acres were even acquired. Captain David L. Stone of the Quartermaster Corps arrived in May 1917 to oversee construction that proceeded at a dizzying rate. The first building was constructed in three days. In 90 days about10,000 men built 1,757 buildings and 422 other structures, lighted, plumbed, and heated. Roads were constructed.

Colonel Peter W. Davison, Commander of the Depot Brigade and the first draftee, Private Herbert W. Hauck, his driver, were the first soldiers to arrive. They were quickly followed by 50,000 enlisted and drafted men.

The determination of the Pierce County leaders can be read on the web page "Camp Lewis 1917-1919" on the Lewis-McChord website. Scan the QR code to read their story. The museum was originally the Red Shield Hotel, built for visitors to the base.

Oct 1, 1917
letter home

Father wants to know how we are mounted. Well most of us are on "Shanks Ponies". There are to be about only 4 horses in our company, 172 men, they are for riding by the upper officers and one of the lower officers who carries messages etc. The guns are pulled by mules and we also have one or two saddle mules. Four companies such as ours makes up the 346th M.G.Bn.

1. Write the definition of "Shanks Ponies" here:

2. How many horses are in the company?

3. How many men?

4. How are guns moved?

5. How many companies make up the 346th M.G.Bn.?

6. What could "M.G. Bn" mean?

Oct 12, 1917
letter home

The drill is getting more difficult both in longer hours and harder to catch on to but they are just that much more interesting. I have found no difficulty as yet in keeping up with all they give us.

Its fun to watch the new hands. But I suppose we were just as green three weeks ago.

There is a school which I attend from 6:30 to 8:00 each night and when that is over it is about time for bed. Wednesdays after-noons and Saturday afternoons and Sunday are about the only days I have much time to write since we drill 8 hours per day.

List what Josh talks about in this section of a letter:

New barracks and base structures constructed at super-speeds.

Notice that in the mess line and in the training post-cards that men are still in civilian clothing.

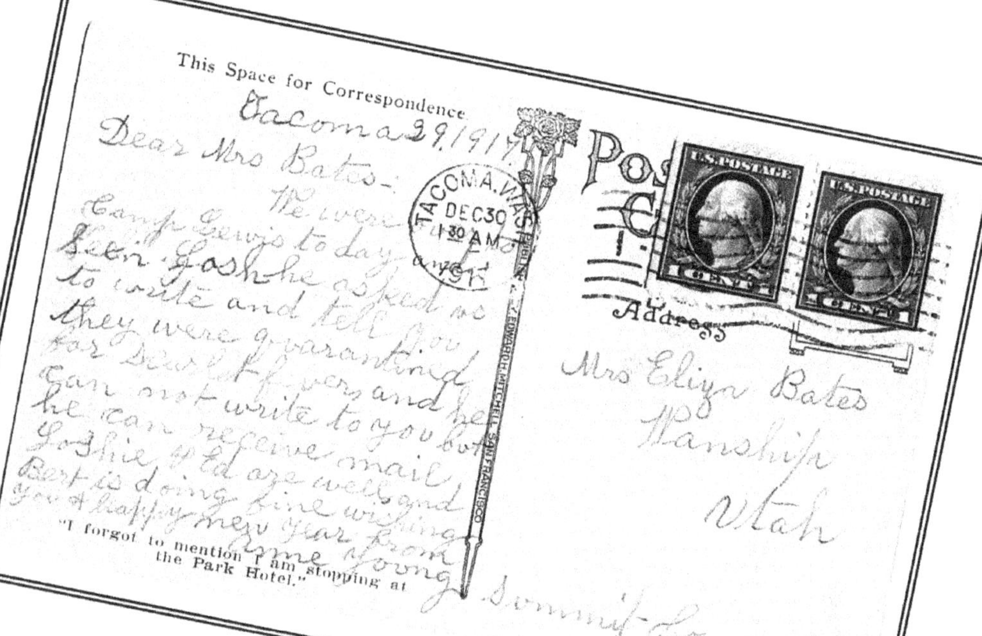

This Space for Correspondence

Tacoma 29/1917

Dear Mrs Bates-

We were at Camp Lewis to day and seen Josh he asked us to write and tell you they were quarantined for Scarlet fever and he can not write to you but he can receive mail. Sophie & Ed are well and Bert is doing fine wishing you a happy new year from Jame Young

"I forgot to mention I am stopping at the Park Hotel."

TACOMA, WASH. DEC 30 1:30 AM 1917

Post Card

Address

Mrs Eliza Bates

Wanship

Summit Co

Utah

A fellow soldier from Utah writes Josh's parents about the reason for the December quarantine.

What is the reason?

____

How much was a stamp?

____

Sunday Nov 4.

On Stable Detail today. Write in afternoon. To foot-ball game in morning. Our team beat. Letter From R.

Monday. Drill most of day. Pay day in afternoon. $42/..

Tuesday Nov. 6, 1917

Detailed to do Clerical work at Base hospital. Letter from Mother & Lilo Bates Candy from Rena. Leave Hospital 10:?? In Bed 10:30

Wednesday Nov. 7

Work to hospital all day, home at 10.45.

Thursday, Work in hospital all day

Friday Nov 9.

Hospital all day write in mornings, before 8:30

Saturday Nov 10

Work a half day. Get a pass and go to Tacoma & Seattle Get a bed at Lincoln Hotel but when I came in after the dance it was taken and I slept in a

Look especially for comments Josh makes about the weather. Why do you think he would pay attention to it?

What kind of work is he doing?

Monday Nov. 26
Work at mustering
office all day.
Tuesday Nov. 27
At office all day
to lecture by captain
also one at assembly
hall by a major
"The field glass & its
use." Rain.
Wednesday Nov 28.
Work half day then
off. Wash shirt.
Get hair cut and
read. Rain.
Thursday Nov 29.
Thanksgiving Day
the first I have not
spent at least

part of it at home.
Mr Powers, Mr Hauck
Mr Able, and myself
eat dinner with a family by the
name of
in Tacoma. Everything
was very nice and
it could of been improved
only by being at
at home. Back to camp
1:30. Rain
Nov 30 Friday.
Work in mustering
office. Stand
muster at barracks
at 1:00. Back again
to mustering office.
weather more pleasant.

Diary on previous page:

What happened on Sunday?

What was the amount of his paycheck as a private?

What is his job assignment?

Did he receive mail? From whom?

What makes this Christmas unusual?

In the margins...what is written?

What does he wonder about those at home?

Tuesday Dec 25.
Xmas and we are quarantined not allowed to leave the barracks. Father was coming to spend it with me but could not on account of the quarantine. Spent the day in reading and writing letters. We have ha big feed at supper tho. The First Xmas that I have not been home for at least part of the day. I wonder how those at home miss me. If I am missed as much as I miss I am sorry in a way yet glad. To bed early after seeing a parade through our barracks by another co.

Rec'd Xmas Package.

Wednesday Dec 26
To work in office all day and at night until 10:00

Thursday Dec. 27
Work during day in barracks at night.

Form 1204

CLASS OF SERVICE	SYMBOL
Day Message	
Day Letter	Blue
Night Message	Nite
Night Letter	N L

If none of these three symbols appears after the check (number of words) this is a day message. Otherwise its character is indicated by the symbol appearing after the check.

WESTERN UNION TELEGRAM

NEWCOMB CARLTON, PRESIDENT GEORGE W. E. ATKINS, FIRST VICE-PRESIDENT

RECEIVED AT COR. PACIFIC AVE. AND 11TH ST., TACOMA, WASH. ALWAYS OPEN

D73FA BF 9

CAMP LEWIS WASH 1237PM JAN 29 1918

JOSHUA BATES SR 125

PARK HOTEL TACOMA WASH

WOULD LIKE TO SEE YOU SOON TODAY AM WELL

JOSHUA

1242PM

1. Origin of the telegram:
2. Date of the telegram:
3. Recipient of the telegram:
4. Delivery destination:
5. Sender of telegram:

6. Time of telegram:

7. Additional information:

8. What proof is there that the meeting occurred?

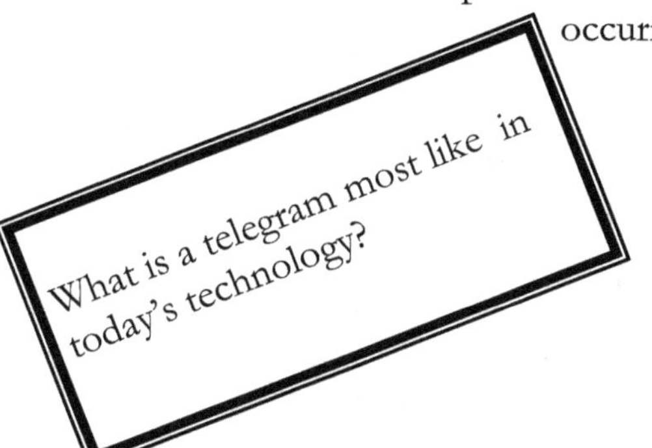

What is a telegram most like in today's technology?

PARK HOTEL — 8th & A Sts.
Opposite Interurban Depot,
TACOMA, WASHINGTON
H.C. Griffith, Propt.
POST CARD
For Correspondence
For Address only
TACOMA, WASH.
1918
Tacoma Wash
Friday Jan 5.
Dear mother,—
Father reached here [illegible]
came over to camp yesterday. [illegible]
I got pass [...] Seattle 11:00 o'c
we are going to Seattle
today. Father's enjoying him
self. Sure seems good to
see him. He is talking to
Mr. Young now in hotel
here. We have been around
large part of Tacoma.
Will write again soon
probably from Seattle
coming back here to-
morrow night. Love from
father and myself,
Josh.
Mrs. Joshua Bates
Wanship
Utah.

Joshua at pup tent

Park Hotel Postcard

I have taken a $50 Liberty Bond
to pay for it $10 a month out of
my wages. I will save that much
anyhow. Probably I could of taken
more. I was glad to hear the receipt
came for my insurance.

Soldiers were encouraged by Secretary McAdoo to buy liberty bonds to help support their families in their absence. How is Josh paying for his?

Josh paid for a $10,000 life insurance policy. How much would that be worth today?

Josh wanted to advance in the Army prior to leaving Camp Lewis. The letter on the following page is from the president of the North Summit School District who was his employer. List the characteristics you learn about Josh in this letter.

Summit
County
State of Utah
JOHN F. WELSH
CHAS. H. WEST
ROY G. LAMBERT
Commissioners
A. C. HORTIN County Clerk
W. S. HORAN Treasurer
P. H. NEELEY Attorney
KATE W. KIMBALL Recorder
A. H. ADDY Assessor
J. D. BIRCH Surveyor
P. F. RYAN Sheriff

Coalville, Utah, Dec. 10th, 1917.

To Whom It May Concern:

Permit me to state, that I am personally acquainted with Mr. Joshua H. Bates of Wanship, Utah, now enlisted in the service of the United States Army, Co."C",346 M.G.Brigade. My acquaintence with Mr. Bates is such that I am able to state that he is a young man of ability and promise in whom full dependence can be placed. He is clean,unadicted to the use of intoxicants or even tobacco, his habits are good and he is a wholesome character.

My acquaintence with him has been over a number of years, and is both private and public. For three years he has taught school in the District over which I am the president, prior to that he was a student in the schools of said district. During all this time his record as a young man of worth was good. When not teaching school or in school, Mr. Bates, like most of our boys in this community worked on his father's ranch. So that I can say that he is looked up to in this neighborhood and his character and record as a man are both good. Any consideration shown him I feel will not be misused.

Respectfully,

County Attorney of Summit County
And President of the Board of
Education of North Summit School
District.

Camp Lewis
Red Cross Convalescent
Home, 1918

What is happening in March 1918?

[illegible]

Thursday Mar 14.
I am up most
of day read &
write. Do not
feel very sick.
Friday Mar 15.
Same as
yesterday. Geo
brings mail
from Barracks
in evening.
Saturday Mar 16
Sunday Mar 17
Monday Mar 18
Tuesday Mar 19
Wednesday Mar 20
Thursday Mar 21
Friday Mar 22

Spent reading &
writing and fuss-
ing around.
Saturday Mar 23
Sunday Mar 24
Monday Mar 25
Tuesday Mar 26
Wednesday Mar 27
Thursday Mar 28
Friday Mar 29

Spent Reading & writing

Saturday Mar 30.
Leave Hospital
to go back to Com-
pany. Lay around
most of day. Fill
tick etc.
Sunday Mar 31.
Easter [illegible]

MACHINE GUN BATTALION
347
COMPANY D

Camp Lewis, Wash
May 12, 1918

Dear Mother and Father, —

"Mother's & Father's Day." I wish I was able to be home to spend it with you. More than ever as I am separated from you by time I realize how good you have been to me. I often wonder if other parents are as good to their children. The guidance you gave me when I was younger was the best that Father and Mother could give. It shall indeed stand me in need now and I must show myself worthy of the trust

What specific comments does Josh make to his parents?

What do you think of his statements? What are your feelings about people who molded you?

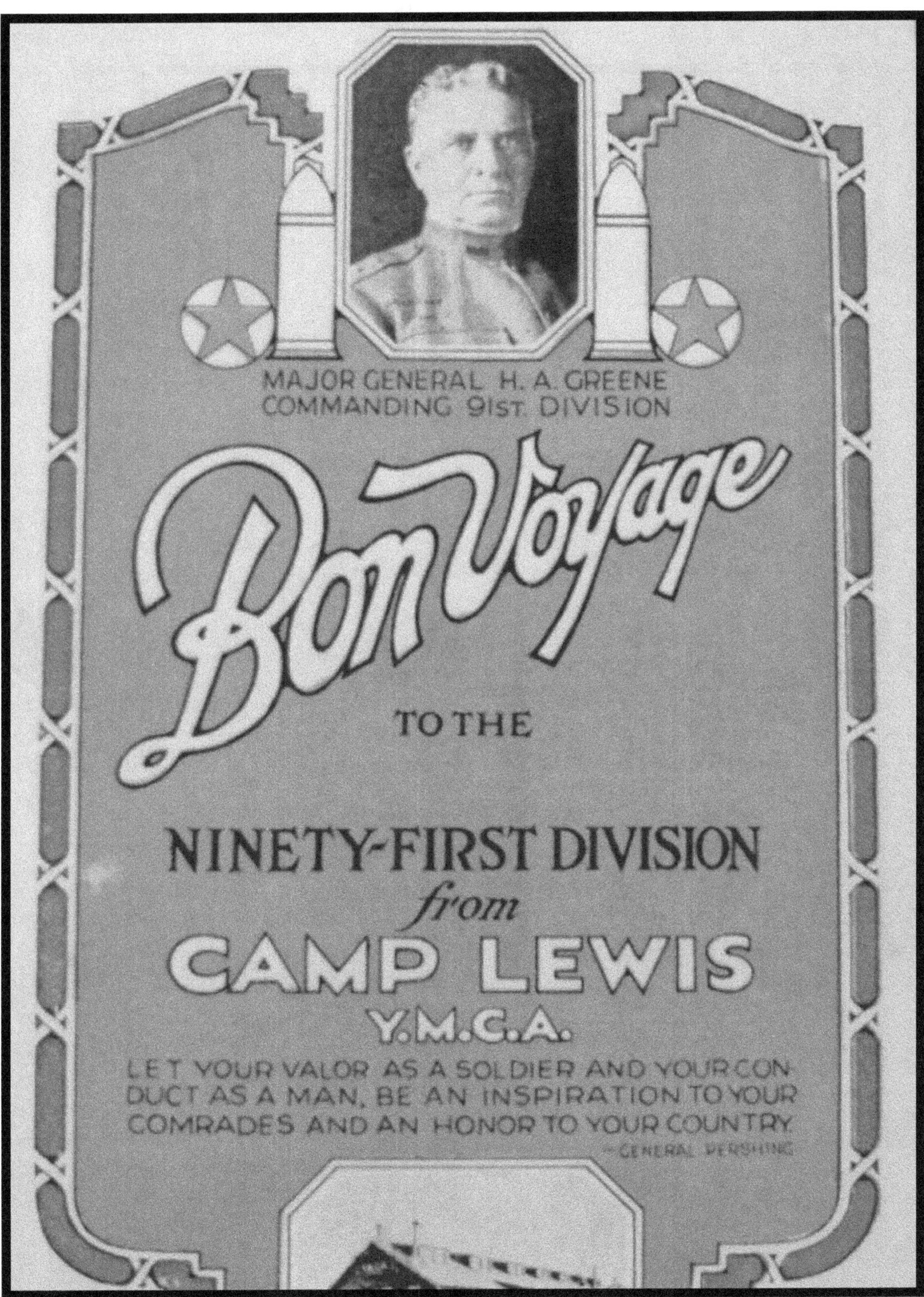
MAJOR GENERAL H. A. GREENE
COMMANDING 91st. DIVISION
Bon Voyage
TO THE
NINETY-FIRST DIVISION
from
CAMP LEWIS
Y.M.C.A.
LET YOUR VALOR AS A SOLDIER AND YOUR CON-
DUCT AS A MAN, BE AN INSPIRATION TO YOUR
COMRADES AND AN HONOR TO YOUR COUNTRY.
—GENERAL PERSHING

Chapter 17: Off to France

WAR WORK COUNCIL

ARMY AND NAVY
YOUNG MEN'S CHRISTIAN ASSOCIATION

"With the Colors"

July 4, 1918 191

evening at night of the same day.

I didnt expect to see New York as soon as I have. It sure is a great City. A person ought to have a two weeks at least, and lots of many.

Well Good-night.
Love and best wishes to all.
May the Lord bless & protect you; from your Loving Son & Brother

Josh.

Address.
Joshua H. Bates
Co. D. 347 M.G. Bn.
American Expeditionary Forces.

This is Josh's last letter from the United States. What is the date? Where is he? What does he think of the area?

COMPANY D, NEAR CHATEAU DE LONNE, MARCH, 1918

A puzzling photograph. Notice the date and the location. Where was Josh in March 1918?
Joshua H. Bates has been identified as the soldier with a tan, 2nd row, between the 6th and 7th men seated in the first row, counting from the left.

Troops line the decks of HMT Ulysses at it pulls out from the wharf at Port Melbourne. . (n.d.). Retrieved April 27, 2016, from https://www.awm.gov.au/collection/PB1095/. This was the transport ship for the 347th to England.

SOLDIERS' MAIL. NO POSTAGE NECESSARY.

THE AMERICAN RED CROSS

MILITARY POST OFFICE

THIS SIDE FOR ADDRESS ONLY.

Mr. & Mrs. Joshua Bates

Summit Co.

THE SHIP ON WHICH I SAILED HAS ARRIVED SAFELY OVERSEAS.

Name Joshua H. Bates

Organization 347 M. G. Bn.

American Expeditionary Forces.

Little is known about this colorful handkerchief. But it is stored with all Joshua's letters and paperwork. We know that it is embroidered and made in France. What is your theory about the handkerchief?

MACHINE GUN BATTALION
347
COMPANY D

Somewhere In France
Aug 14, 1918

Dear Brother and All at Home—

As yet we are continuing our training in the same place. Weather conditions have been fine the last week and prospects of more of it.

I suppose by this time you have the "haying" about done. How did you get along. Hired help was very scarce I suppose. No doubt it was up to Father you & Roy. Grain will be

1

Herald but it does not give us a great deal of the news from America so tell everything you can think of in the line of news when you write. We have had as yet but the one delivery of mail but expect more in the near future.

Love and best wishes to all.
From Broth & Son
Josh

Will be waiting for a bunch of letters for some more news of the Home town and those there.

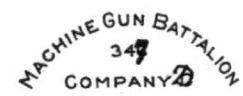

Joshua H. Bates (2,253,462)
Co. D. 347 M. G. Bn.
American E. F.
A.P.O. 776.

O.K.
Arthur E. Carlson
2nd Lt. Inf. R.C.

3

The previous page shows a letter to Josh's brother Parley, the Parley that he tried to find in Salt Lake City the summer of 1917. The letter only shows pages 1 and 3. Below is the envelop.

Look carefully to see what is distinctive about the letter and envelop. It is not the content. What is distinctive? What is the importance of it?

Your answer:

Chapter 18: Meuse-Argonne Offensive

Read this about the 347th. Questions follow.

24 HISTORY OF THE 347th

the early afternoon of this day Company C laid down a special barrage preparatory to a determined attack upon Gesnes, the 362nd Infantry leading the attack and employing its own machine gun company and Company C of our battalion, and the 361st Infantry being in close support with Companies A and D of this battalion. Company B had been placed in combat liaison with the 37th Division on our right.

The advance upon Gesnes was the most intense and severe action which the 181st Brigade experienced. The greater part of our casualties in the Meuse-Argonne Offensive occurred that afternoon. Troops of our brigade drove the Germans in front of them and entered and outposted the town, Major Hanson being for a time in command of the situation. We were later ordered to withdraw to a commanding position on hills a kilometer and a half south of Gesnes.

Troops of the 181st Brigade remained in substantially this position from September 30 until they were relieved on the night of October 3, Company A occupying the left of the sector for a time, Company D the center, later taking over the sector of Company A also, and Company B on the right. Our guns were placed well up in the front lines with the infantry. On September 30, Companies A and C were attached to the 362nd Infantry, which was placed in support of the 182nd Brigade.

This period of holding the line was one of comparative inactivity, which held its disadvantages for us, none the less. We were compelled to take the enemy's unceasing shell-fire while doing nothing in return, the hardest thing a soldier has to do.

It was at this time that we received our first replacements—twenty-three in number.

On October 3 we were relieved by the machine gunners of the 32nd Division, and moved back after dark to a position on the northwest edge of the Bois de Very. We were looking forward to a period of rest and of recuperation from the dysentery which had become very prevalent in the ranks, but we were instead detached from the 91st Division and placed under the control of the First Army Corps. With some disgust, because of our weakened condition, we saw the other brigade of our division go back to a rest area, while we went forward again on the night of October 7, to the front line in the sector to the west of that formerly occupied. Our position here was somewhat further advanced, being approximately abreast of Gesnes and north of Eclisfontaine and the Trousol Farm.

At this time the 181st Brigade was attached to the 1st Division and was given a narrow sector between the 32nd Division on the right and the 1st Division on the left. During the next four days the lines were advanced to include the Bois-de-Chensec and hills 269 and 255. The troops on October 11 met with stiff machine gun resistance from well fortified enemy positions on hill 288, but succeeded in overcoming it. On that date, too,

Calkins, J. Uberto. (1919). *History of the 347th machine gun battalion: Compiled from official records and the personal notes of various members of the battalion.* Oakland [Calif.]: Horwinsk

BRIGADIER GENERAL J. B. McDONALD
Commanding the 181st Infantry Brigade. Photographed in the Argonne

Calkins, J. Uberto. (1919). *History of the 347th machine gun battalion: Compiled from official records and the personal notes of various members of the battalion.* Oakland [Calif.]: Horwinsk

Using the excerpt from the history of the 347th on the previous page, answer these questions about the 2nd battle of the Meuse-Argonne campaign.

1. Which battle was the most intense that the 181st Brigade experienced?

2. What days were the Brigade in their conquered position?

3. What part of the line did Company D occupy?

4. Were companies A, B, C, and D of the 91st Division active or holding?

5. What was the enemy doing during this time?

6. When did the 32nd Division appear and why?

7. What was the plan for the Brigade in the immediate future?

8. What happened to the 347th?

91st Division, American Expeditionary Force, World War I http://www.newrivernotes.com/ww1/91divaef.htm

HEADQUARTERS FIFTH ARMY CORPS
American Expeditionary Forces

France, 3rd October, 1918.

From: Commanding General, V Army Corps.
To: Commanding General, 91st Division.

Subject: Relief of 91st Division.

Under orders from the First Army, the 91st Division will be relieved from the front line tonight and placed in Corps Reserve.

The Corps Commander wishes you to understand that this relief results solely from a realization by higher command that your Division has done its full share in the recent success, and is entitled to a rest for reorganization. This especially as, during the past three days, it has incurred heavy casualties when circumstances would not permit either advance or withdrawal.

At a time when the divisions on its flanks were faltering and even falling back, the 91st pushed ahead and steadfastly clung to every yard gained.

In its initial performance, your Division has established itself firmly in the list of the Commander-in-Chief's reliable fighting units. Please extend to your officers and men my appreciation of their splendid behavior and my hearty congratulations on the brilliant record they have made.

GEORGE H. CAMERON,
Major General, Commanding.

In the next few pages, discover how this order affects Josh.

1. Who wrote this order?
2. To whom is it addressed?
3. What is the subject?
4. What is to happen?
5. Why is it to happen?
6. What compliments are given?
7. Who signed the order?
8. Find an article in Wikipedia about this person.
9. What is the date of this order?

Private Joshua H. Bates of company D was killed on October 4. He had just brought up a message that company D had been relieved, and he was very cheerful over the fact that the long period of holding the line day and night under shellfire was about to end, for a time at least. A machine gun unit from the 32nd division, which was just marching in to relieve the right wing of the 91st, was to replace the 347th machine gun battalion. The infantry of the 181st brigade, in fact, had for the most part marched out on the night before, having been relieved by 32nd division infantry. Private Bates was just going into a dugout to report having called in a part of a company D platoon that he had been ordered to bring, preparatory to its going back. Suddenly a pair of bracket shells came. Private Bates was struck by a fragment high up in the chest and died practically instantly. All he said was, "Oh". This happened in the southeast corner of the Bois de Baulny, about half a mile across the opening from the Bois de Cierges. Private Bates was buried where he fell. An eyewitness of his death was Sergeant Frank Bedell, of Golconda, Nev., who was lying beside him at the time. "Private Bates was an exceptionally conscientious and cheerful soldier,—a high class man," said Captain Thomas. He was the last man killed before the 347th machine gun battalion was relieved for the first time.

List the details regarding Joshua on October 4, 191 8.

1. Cancellation dates of parents' three letters:
2. Stamp says:
3. Written note says:

If none of these three symbols appears after the check (number of words) this is a telegram. Otherwise its character is indicated by the symbol appearing after the check.

TELEGRAM

NEWCOMB CARLTON, PRESIDENT GEORGE W. E. ATKINS, FIRST VICE-PRESIDENT

If none of these three symbols appears after the check (number of words) this is a telegram. Otherwise its character is indicated by the symbol appearing after the check.

RECEIVED AT SX KI 33 Government

WA. Washington D.C. 405 PM Nov 6th 1918.

Mr.Joshawa Bates.

Wanship Summit County Utah.

Deeply regret to infor m you that private Joshuah Bates machine gun Batallion is officially reported as Killed in action October fourth,

Harris.The Adjutant Genrral.

2.50.pm.

Phoned 3.02 pm 11/6/18

Form 116.

Western Union Telegraph Co.

INCORPORATED.

CABLE SERVICE TO ALL PARTS OF THE WORLD.

Pay no Charges to Messenger unless written in Ink in Delivery Bo

Mr. Joshuah Bates.
Wanship Utah

No.

Charges

Information included in this telegram:
1. Date sent:
2. From:
3. To:
4. Who has been killed in action?
5. What was the date of death?
6. Where did the telegram originate?

What questions or concerns do you have about the telegram?

Mortuary Notice

Date: Wednesday, November 13, 1918 **Paper:** Salt Lake Telegram (Salt Lake City, Utah) **Page:** 5

Joshua Bates, Wanship, Utah, is reported killed in action on today's casualty list.

Killed in action, 310.
Died of wounds, 100.
Died of accident and other causes, 14.
Died of airplane accident, 2.
Died in sinking, 1.
Died of disease, 189.
Wounded severely, 90.
Wounded, degree undetermined, 159.
Wounded slightly, 105.
Missing in action, 78.
Prisoners, 13.
Total, 1061.

KILLED IN ACTION.

Lieutenants—

Samuel Tyler Adams, Caldwell, Ida.
Truman A. Starr, Seattle, Wash.

Privates—

Vancenzo Albi, Denver, Colo.
Anthony Altman, Spokane, Wash.
JOSHUA H. BATES, WANSHIP, SUMMIT COUNTY, UTAH.
James K. McCallum, Dixon, Mont.
Christian A. Rasmussen, Fresno, Cal

Why is Joshua's name all capitalized?

Letter to Mr. Joshua Bates from Captain Edwin S. Thomas, Company D, 347th Machine Gun Battalion, December 4, 1918.

Copy of Capt Thomas' letter which we received after Joshua's death

Co. "D" 347 M. G. Bn.
American E. F. A.P.O. #776
December. 4, 1918.

Mr. Joshua Bates,
Wansley, Utah.

Dear Mr. Bates:-

You have probably heard from the War Department of the death of your son, Joshua H. Bates, near Fresnes, on October, 3th 1918.

The high regard that I held for your son both as a soldier and a gentleman prompts me to write to you and communicate what information I can as to the manner of his death. He was killed by shell fire while in the performance of his duty, in fact while taking a message of relief to one of the isolated platoons of the company.

You have every reason to be proud of your son for the way in which he upheld the best traditions of the American Army in France.

His cheerfulness and willingness to do his duty under the most trying circumstances were especially

How did Captain Thomas describe Josh?

Thomas, Page 2

marked and his death was a severe
loss to the company.
I am sending you a tracing
showing where he was killed and later
buried by the Chaplain. You can
locate the grave by reference to the
"Verdun A" map, scale 1/20,000, by super-
imposing the tracing of that map.
May I extend my deep sympathy
in this great loss you have suffered
for the cause of world peace, and for
the country that we serve.

Very sincerely,
Edwin S. Thomas,
Capt. 347, M. G. Bn.
Comdg. Co. "D."

Why do you feel that Thomas has reliable information about Josh's death?

Locate Gesnes, Bois Communal de Baulney and Bois Communal de Cierges on the Google Earth map based on the Army cartographer's tracing below. Locate Joshua's first gravesite on both maps.

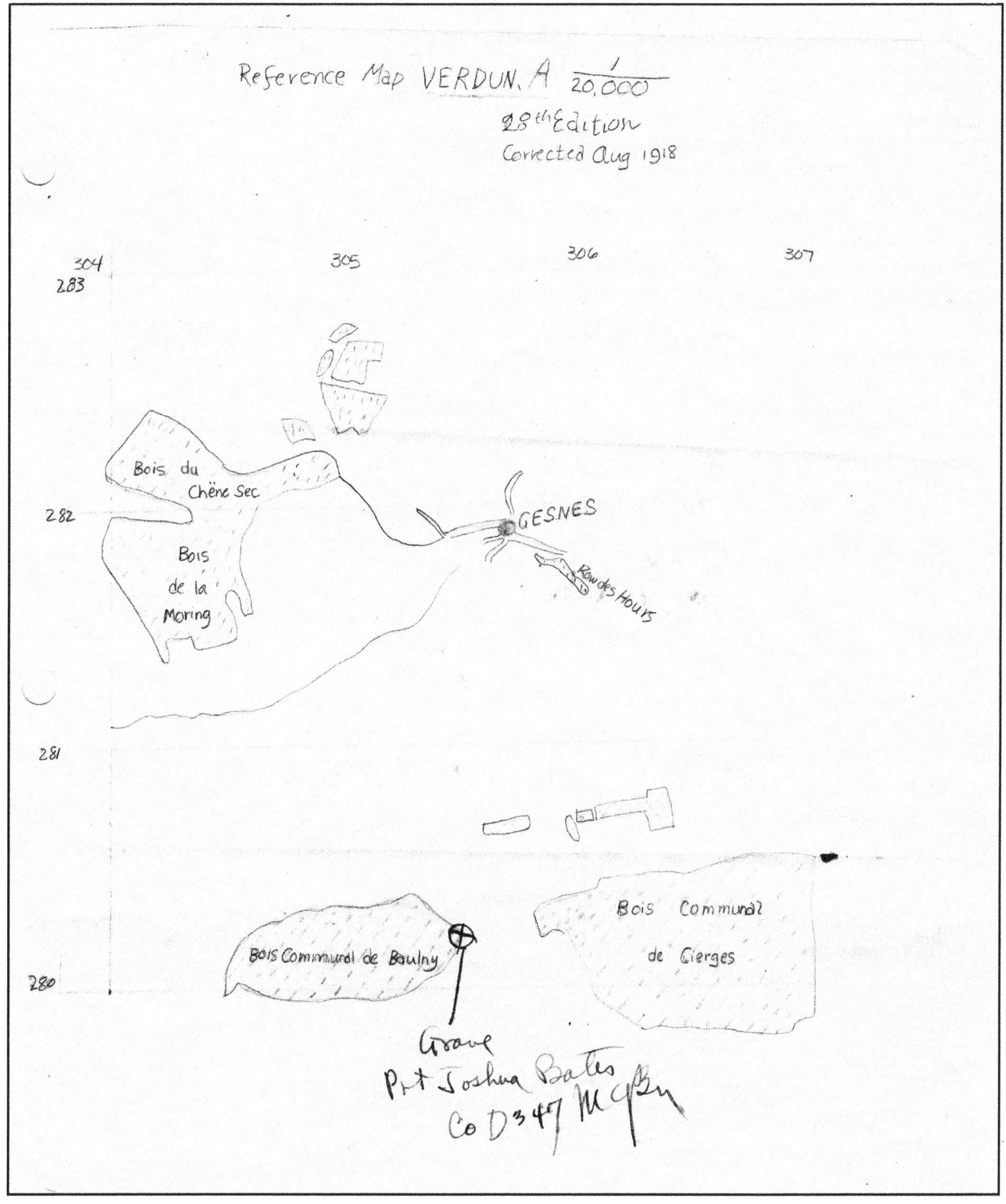

Gesnes-en-Argonne
Exermont, France
Exermont
Apremont
© 2007 Europa Technologies
© 2007 Cnes/Spot Image
Google
Eye alt 26817 ft

Letter to Mrs. Joshua Bates from Lieutenant H. W. Price, Company D,

Dec. 21, 1918
Mesves, France,

My dear Mrs. Bates:

Your letter asking for information of your son Joshua was forwarded to me here where I am in a hospital recovering from wounds received September twenty ninth while attacking the village of Gesnes. This village is a few miles northwest from Montfaucon.

This was the fourth day of the advance in the Argonne and I saw Joshua less than an hour before I was wounded. At that time he was well and happy. That is the latest news I can give you of him as I have been away from the company since that day.

I have known your son ever since he arrived at Camp Lewis, fifteen months ago and know him to be an honest, loyal and upright young man. As a soldier he was faithful, courageous and well disciplined. I had occasion to take him with me as a messenger two days before I was wounded on a

-2-

mission which entailed our passing thru a great deal of shell-fire. We passed thru this danger alright and he rendered invaluable assistance in carrying messages to the company and battalion headquarters.

The day on which I was wounded my platoon was acting independently so he was not with me as his work lay with the company headquarters.

I am forwarding your letter to the company as they can give you later information of him.

I sincerely hope that the report that he was killed was incorrect. It is a shame that so many of our fine young men had to give up their lives. If, however it proves true, please accept my deepest sympathy and remember that as a soldier, as a man, and as a son he was one to be proud of.

Very sincerely

Lt. H.W. Price,

347th M. G. Bn.

A.P.O. 776, American E. F

Questions on the following page delve into the details of the letter, which talks about Joshua's character as well as some assignments and missions.

Piecing Together Information from Lieutenant Price's Letter

1. What was the date this officer last saw Josh?
2. How long has the officer known Josh?
3. List all the words this officer uses to describe Josh.
4. What role did Josh play with this officer?
5. What was their goal in the mission when they were under a great amount of shell fire?
6. Where was Josh on the day this officer was wounded?
7. Who was this officer?
8. How current was his information compared to Captain Thomas's?

MAJOR McCAUSTLAND AND STAFF
Major Swanson, Captains Price, Thomas and Barrows, and Lieutenants Olmstead, Brookes and Davis

Calkins

Form No. 364

NATIONAL OFFICERS
WOODROW WILSON, PRESIDENT
ROBERT W. DE FOREST, VICE-PRESIDENT
WILLIAM HOWARD TAFT, VICE-PRESIDENT
JOHN SKELTON WILLIAMS, TREASURER
ALEXANDER C. KING, COUNSELOR
MISS MABEL T. BOARDMAN, SECRETARY

THE AMERICAN RED CROSS
NATIONAL HEADQUARTERS
WASHINGTON, D. C.

DEPARTMENT OF COMMUNICATION
W. R. CASTLE, JR., DIRECTOR

EXECUTIVE COMMITTEE
FRANKLIN K. LANE
MERRITTE W. IRELAND
WILLIAM C. BRAISTED
HENRY P. DAVISON
ELIOT WADSWORTH
MRS. AUGUST P. BELMONT
GEORGE E. SCOTT

LIVINGSTON FARRAND, CHAIRMAN
WILLOUGHBY G. WALLING, VICE-CHAIRMAN
FREDERICK P. KEPPEL, VICE-CHAIRMAN

FREDERICK C. MUNROE, GENERAL MANAGER

To the Relatives of Our American Dead:

The Red Cross desires to give you certain information concerning photographs of graves which are being given to relatives of our American dead.

The Red Cross has carried on the work of photographing and distributing these pictures by authority and under the direction of the Graves Registration Service of the Army. It should be understood, however, that the Red Cross has nothing whatever to do with location of graves, the disposition of bodies, or the inscriptions on the crosses. All correspondence on these matters should be addressed to Colonel Charles C. Pierce, Chief, Graves Registration Service, Washington, D. C.

Three copies of each photograph of a soldier's grave are being sent to his next of kin or emergency addressee. According to the records of the Adjutant General's Office, the Graves Registration Service and the Red Cross, you are the person entitled to receive the enclosed pictures. Neither time nor pains have been spared in our cooperative effort to insure the utmost accuracy. It is possible, however, that among a large number of men with similar or identical names an occasional confusion in address will occur. If by any chance these photographs do not belong to you please return them at once in order that they may be sent if possible, to their correct destination.

Should the picture you are now receiving show the location of the grave to be different from the one stated in the official notice originally sent you, you are assured that this is due to the fact that a great many transfers have been made to selected cemeteries where bodies can be more satisfactorily cared for; and that an error in the inscription on the cross or a difference in location of the grave concerning which you have not as yet been officially notified in no way affects the identity of the dead. The number at the bottom of the photograph has no relation to the grave number at the top of the cross, but serves merely to identify the photograph.

More than three prints cannot be supplied by the Red Cross, but any reliable photographer can make copies from those which are enclosed. The blank spaces on the folder have been left for you to fill in as you may desire.

The Graves Registration Service and the American Red Cross will be amply repaid for long months of arduous labor if you accept these photographs as a reverent tribute to the American soldier who made the supreme sacrifice.

1. How many items will the Red Cross provide to a family?

2. When will the items arrive?

3. What are these items?

The American Red Cross

National Headquarters

Washington, D.C.

With deep sympathy in your loss

The American Red Cross

sends you the photograph of the grave of

this American Soldier

who gave his life for his country

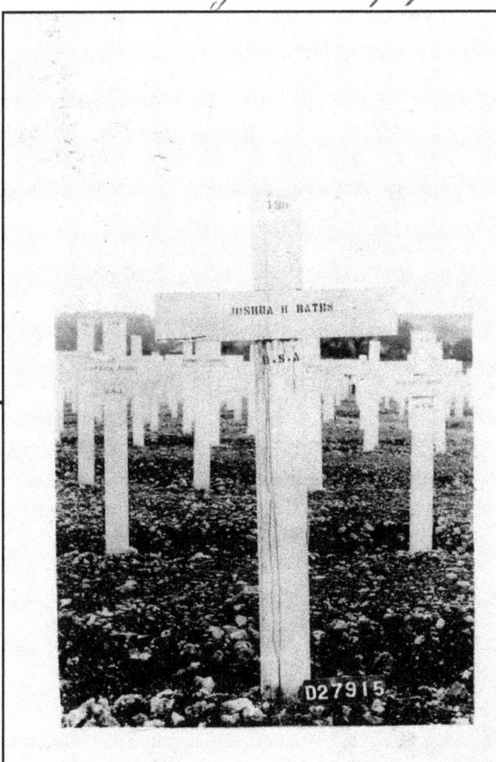

Was this Josh's first burial?

The Meuse-Argonne American Cemetery is about twenty-five miles north of Verdun. These grounds have the largest amount of American soldier graves in Europe.

Josh's temporary grave and temporary cross with "Joshua H. Bates" was here until the family requested repatriation.

Visit the Meuse-Argonne American Cemetery.

PERSY STANFORT AUBREY (2255483), Private - Box 188, Park City, Utah

Enlisted at Park City, Utah, September 19, 1917; joined Battalion March 15, 1918, at Camp Lewis, Washington. Appointed Private, first class, October 21, 1918. Actions engaged in: St. Mihiel, Meuse-Argonne, Ypres-Lys.

ALFRED D. AUSTIN (2255485), Private first class - Paradise Valley, Nevada

Enlisted September 19, 1917, at Winnemucca, Nevada; joined Battalion March 15, 1918, at Camp Lewis, Washington. Actions engaged in: St. Mihiel, Meuse-Argonne. Evacuated to hospital on account of wounds received in action September 29, 1918.

FRANKLIN AUSTIN (2255442), Sergeant - - - - Sixteen, Montana

Enlisted September 19, 1917, at White Sulphur Springs, Montana; joined Battalion March 15, 1918, at Camp Lewis, Washington. Appointed Corporal December 6, 1917; Sergeant January 18, 1918. Actions engaged in: St. Mihiel, Meuse-Argonne. Attended Division Gas School at Camp Lewis, Washington. Attended Army Candidates' School at La Valbonne, France.

HARRY ARTHUR BAGWELL (3440447), Private - - - - - -
2215 North Thirty-second St., East St. Louis, Illinois

Enlisted June 15, 1918, at East St. Louis, Illinois; joined Battalion October 21, 1918, at Roulers, Belgium. Actions engaged in: Ypres-Lys.

JOSEPH RALPH BAILEY (4000229), Private - R. F. D. 2, Peterson, Iowa

Enlisted July 24, 1918, at Pringhar, Iowa; joined Battalion November 4, 1918, Belgium. Actions engaged in: Ypres-Lys.

HARRY EARL BATES (2933578), Private, first class - - - - - -
726 S. Eighth St., Cambridge, Ohio

Enlisted June 23, 1918, at Caldwell, Ohio; joined Battalion October 21, 1918, at Roulers, Belgium. Appointed Private, first class, December 1, 1918. Actions engaged in: Ypres-Lys.

JAMES ERRIC BATES (2933844), Private - - Sweet Chalybate, Virginia

Enlisted June 26, 1918, at Alliance, Ohio; joined Battalion October 21, 1918, at Roulers, Belgium. Actions engaged in: Ypres-Lys.

JOSHUA A. BATES (2255462), Private, first class - - Wanship, Utah

Enlisted September 19, 1917, at Park City, Utah. Appointed Private, first class, December 1, 1917; joined Battalion March 15, 1918, at Camp Lewis, Washington. Actions engaged in: St. Mihiel, Meuse-Argonne. Killed in action October 3, 1918. Cited for gallantry in action by G. O. 6, Headquarters Ninety-first Division, January 2, 1919.

FRANK BEDELL (2255455), Sergeant - - - - - Golconda, Nevada

Enlisted at Winnemucca, Nevada, September 18, 1917. Appointed Corporal December 6, 1917; joined Battalion March 15, 1918. Appointed Sergeant June 10, 1918. Actions engaged in: St. Mihiel, Meuse-Argonne, Ypres-Lys.

LAVERN B. BEESON (2255435), Sergeant. - - - - - Lovelock, Nevada

Enlisted at Lovelock, Nevada, September 18, 1917. Appointed Corporal Octo-

Calkins, J. Uberto. (1919). *History of the 347th machine gun battalion: Compiled from official records and the personal notes of various members of the battalion.* Oakland [Calif.]: Horwinsk

In which battles was Josh?

For what was he cited?

COMMENDATION

(280—FOR OFFICIAL CIRCULATION ONLY)

Headquarters 91st Division, A. E. F., October 4, 1918.

GENERAL ORDERS NO. 24.

1. The following letter which has just been received from the Commanding General, 5th Corps, is published for the information of all concerned. It is a source of great gratification to the Division Commander that the division in its initial fight acquitted itself in such a creditable manner as to bring forth this letter from the Corps Commander:

HEADQUARTERS FIFTH ARMY CORPS,
American Expeditionary Forces,
France, October 3, 1918.

From: Commanding General V Army Corps.
To: Commanding General 91st Division.
Subject: Relief of 91st Division.

Under orders from First Army, the 91st Division will be relieved from the front line tonight and placed in Corps Reserve.

The Corps Commander wishes you to understand that this relief results solely from a realization by higher command that your division has done its full share in the recent success, and is entitled to a rest for reorganization. This especially as during the past three days it has incurred heavy casualties when circumstances would not permit either advance or withdrawal.

At a time when the divisions on its flanks were faltering and even falling back, the Ninety-first pushed ahead and steadfastly clung to every yard gained.

In its initial performance, your division has established itself firmly on the list of the Commander-in-Chief's reliable fighting units. Please extend to your officers and men my appreciation of their splendid behavior and my hearty congratulations on the brilliant record they have made.

GEO. H. CAMERON,
Major General, Commanding.

BY COMMAND OF MAJOR GENERAL JOHNSTON.

H. J. Brees,
Colonel, General Staff.
Chief of Staff.

OFFICIAL:
(D. J. Coman)
Major, A. G.
Acting Adjutant.

Calkins, J. Uberto. (1919). *History of the 347th machine gun battalion: Compiled from official records and the personal notes of various members of the battalion.* Oakland [Calif.]: Horwinsk

For what is the 91st Division praised?

Chapter 20: Coming Home

Summit County Boy Dies For World Liberty

(Special Correspondence.)

WANSHIP, Summit Co., Nov. 20.—Mr. and Mrs. Joshua Bates have a telegram from the war department announcing the death of their son, Private Joshua H. Bates.

JOSHUA H. BATES.

Private Bates went to Camp Lewis in September, 1917, where he received his training. He was a member of the 347th machine gun battalion. He landed in France July 23, 1918. The telegram stated he was killed Oct. 4, while operating his machine gun.

Private Bates was a native of Wanship and was 23 years of age. He was a graduate of the North Summit high school. He studied two summers at the University of Utah and for two years was principal of the Wanship school. He leaves a father, mother, three brothers and two sisters.

Yes, you have seen this obituary before, in Chapter 2. Did you realize that newspapers are considered secondary sources? That means that the person writing the story is at least two times removed from the actual facts. Josh's journal? That was a primary source as the primary person wrote for two years about his activities and work and romance. If his brother Parley wrote about Josh's activities, even though he knows Josh well, the book would be a secondary source.

So after that discussion, I have changed my mind. This obituary is at least three times removed, a tertiary source. The information was given to the paper by someone other than Josh, and the news writer then wrote the obituary.

Now to the point of this page. You have read extensively about Josh's life and death.

1.

2.

3.

4.

5.

6.

The Bateses could choose to send his mother, Eliza Bates, to France to view his grave, or choose to have his body exhumed and brought to Utah for burial at home. How is the telegram proof of their choice?

Form 1201

CLASS OF SERVICE	SYMBOL
Day Message	
Day Letter	Blue
Night Message	Nite
Night Letter	N L

If none of these three symbols appears after the check (number of words) this is a day message. Otherwise its character is indicated by the symbol appearing after the check.

WESTERN UNION TELEGRAM

NEWCOMB CARLTON, PRESIDENT GEORGE W. E. ATKINS, FIRST VICE-PRESIDENT

RECEIVED AT

SY KI 19 Govt.

y Hoboken N J 240 PM sept 3

Joshua Bates,

summit county wanship Utah.

remains private first class Joshua P Bates leave Jersey city september third midnight arrive wanship utah via union Pacific Railroad.

Graves Registeration service.

4pm.

Form 2982. E. 6-1

UNION PACIFIC RAILROAD CO.

TELEGRA

J Bates
Wanship

This Envelope is to be used for delivery of Tele

Original certificate, in the J. Lambert Bates collection, son of A Parley Bates, 2013

This enlargement of a small amateur photograph is the only known one of his burial.
What number is this burial?

Explain "double exposure."

List other technology of the Progressive Era that are mentioned in other chapters of this book.

This is Josh's headstone in the Wanship Cemetery of Wanship, Summit, Utah.

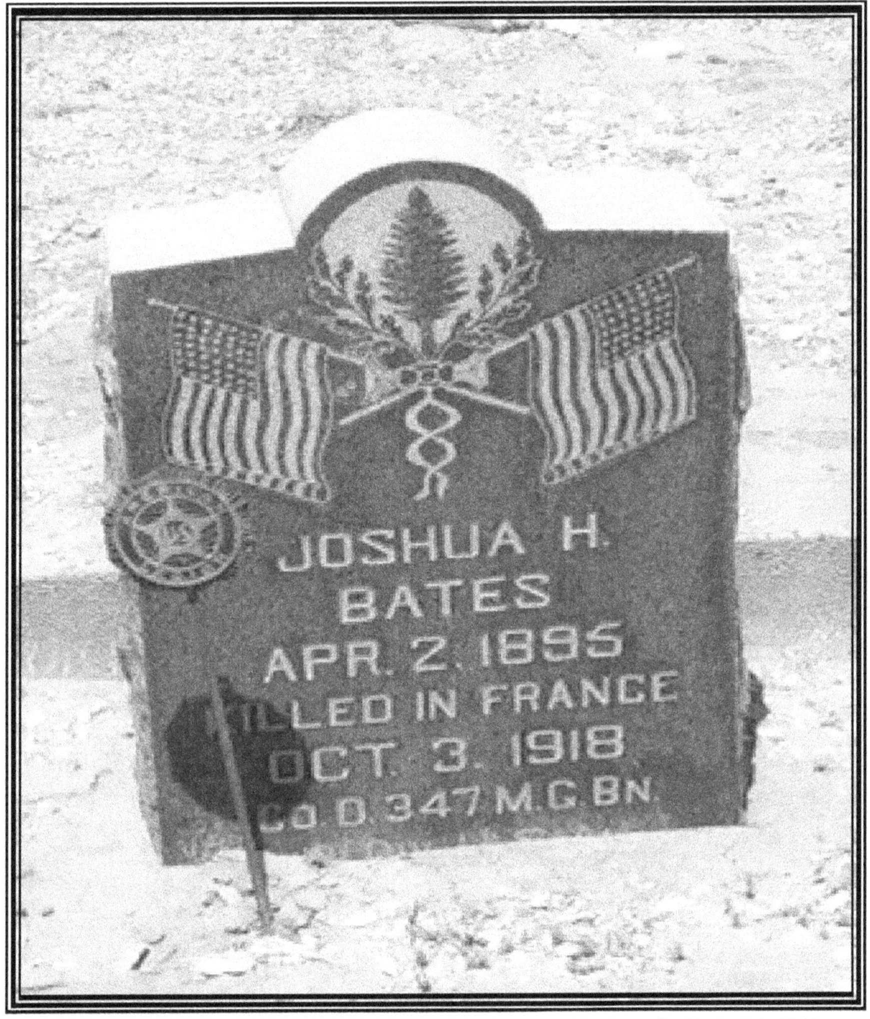

Photograph by Janet Brinton Dreyer, Wanship Cemetery, Wanship, Summit , Utah,. July 2012.

Many people transcribe the information on headstones for large online indexes of graves. Two are "Find-a-Grave" and "BillionGraves."

First the transcriber takes a photograph of the headstone with a smart phone that also records the GPS. Then he or she logs into their account where the photographs are stored and transcribes the information accurately into the database so that family anywhere in the world can search for birth and death information for their loved ones.

Transcribe Josh's information here:

1. Full name ______________________________

2. Birth date ______________________________

3. Death date______________________________

4. Other engravings __________________________

5. Observations ____

6. What is the meaning of the evergreen tree? _____________________________

Insight: What About Rena?

We know that Joshua and Rena were committed to each other. She visited him each day of his illness the winter of 1917. He courted her despite the ups and downs of their relationship. She faithfully wrote him letters during his training and service.

Rena grieved Joshua's death and vowed never to marry. The vow must have been serious as both her parents and Josh's parents counseled her to reconsider.

Rena eventually did marry… a young man from a neighboring town, from the Brinton family. A life of synchronicity. She lost a Bates, but gained a Brinton. More information about that will come.

Summit Co. Pass

UTAH STATE HISTORICAL SOCIETY
STATE CAPITOL, SALT LAKE CITY

WAR SERVICE QUESTIONNAIRE

I.

GENERAL

Name of Person in Service Joshua H. Bates
Home Address Wanship, Summit Co. Ut.
Camp or Oversea Address Co. D 347 M. G. Bn.
A. E. F.
Date of Birth Apr. 2, 1895 Place Wanship, Utah
White or Colored White
Parents { Mother Eliza P. Bates
{ Father Joshua Bates
Education Grammer grade, High school graduate
One year credit at University of Utah.
Two years successful teaching in the state of Utah. Active member of L. D. S. Church.
Occupation or Profession Before Entering Service School teaching and farming
Name of Employer Self
Address of Employer
Married? If Married Give Name of Wife
Number of Children Names of Children:

Bates, Joshua H.

Utah State Archives and Records Service, Salt Lake City, Utah; *Military Service Cards, ca. 1898-1975*; Creating Agency: *Department of Administrative Services, Division of Archives and Records Service*, Series: *85268*; Reel: *2*

V.

CASUALTIES

Killed in Action:
Date Oct. 3, 1918 Place Meuse-Argonne
Died of Disease:
Disease
Date Place
Wounded in Action:
Date Place
Nature of Wounds
Prisoners:
Date Place
Died of Accident and Other Causes:
Date Place
Details

Remarks: Killed while delivering a message of relief to an isolate platoon.

Mr. & Mrs. Joshua Bates father & mother
Signature of person who fills out questionnaire

NOTE.—Send photograph. Record will be incomplete without photograph. Enclose interesting incidents, clippings, letters and other material which should be made part of record. Don't neglect this opportunity to have your boy properly represented on the permanent records of Utah.

D. W. PARRATT, Secretary.

Additional information about Josh discovered in the forms from the War Service Questionnaire:

II.

INDUCTION

Date of Induction Into Service Sept. 19, 1917

Method of Induction (a) Selective X (b) Volunteer

Branch of Service (Army) X (Navy) (Marines)

Name and Number of Company and Regiment Co. D 347 M. G. Bn.

Division 91st

Commanding Officer Major J. C. McCaustland 347 Machine Gun Battalion

If in Navy—Name of Ship

Other Organizations He Has Belonged to

Name of First Training Camp Camp Lewis, Washington

Name of Other Training Camps

Time Spent in Each Camp 9 mo at Camp Lewis

Remarks:

III.

OVERSEA SERVICE

Date of Transportation Overseas July 5, 1918

Place of Oversea Service France

Remarks: Attended school in France. Actions engaged in: St Mihiel, Meuse-Argonne

IV.

PROMOTIONS

Rank at Entrance Into Service Private

Previous Military Training

Promotions, with Date of Each First class private December 1, 1917

If Discharged, Give Date

Citations for Bravery, etc. Cited for gallantry in action by G. O. C. Headquarters Ninety-first Division, January 2, 1919.

Remarks:

Bates, Josphua H. 2,255,462 * White
(Surname) (Christian name) (Army serial number)

Residence: XXX Wanship Summit UTAH
(Street and house number) (Town or city) (County) (State)

* Inducted at Park City Utah on Sept 19, 1917

Place of birth: Wanship Utah Age or date of birth: 22 6/12 Yrs

Organizations served in, with dates of assignments and transfers: Co C 346 MG Bn Oct 4/17 to Mch 15/18; Co D 347 MG Bn to Oct 4/18;

Grades, with date of appointment: Pvt Sept 19/17 Pvt 1 cl Dec 1/17

Engagements: Argonne, St Mihiel

Served overseas from July 6/18 to † Oct 4/18 from † to †

Killed in action October 4, 1918

Other wounds or injuries received in action: None (If none, so state)

Person notified of death: Joshua Bates (Name) Father (Degree of relationship) Wanship, Summit County, Utah
(No. and street or rural route) (City, town, or post office) (State or country)

Remarks:

Form No. 724-6, A. G. O. Nov. 22, 1919. * Strike out words not applicable. † Dates of departure from and arrival in the U. S.

Utah State Archives and Records Service; Salt Lake City, Utah; *World War I Service Questionnaires, 1914-1918*; Creating Agency: *State Historical Society*; Series: *85298*; Reel: *2*

NAME BATES, JOSHUA H. SERIAL NUMBER [illegible]

RANK Pvt. 1/cl ORGANIZATION Co. D 347 MG Bn 91 Div. BRANCH Army

PERIOD OF SERVICE World War I

DATE OF ENLISTMENT 19 Sept. 1917 PLACE Park City, Utah

DATE OF DISCHARGE 4 Oct. 1918 KIA PLACE [illegible]

DATE OF BIRTH 2 April 1895 PLACE Wanship, Utah

DATE OF DEATH 4 Oct. 1918 PLACE France

PLACE OF BURIAL CITY Wanship COUNTY Summit

CEMETERY City PLOT LOCATION

NEXT OF KIN Joshua Bates ADDRESS Wanship, Utah RELATIONSHIP Father

REMARKS:

MARKER Yes DATE VERIFIED

BATES, JOSHUA H. SUMMIT CO. WANSHIP CITY

LARSON, ANDREW F. SUMMIT CO. WANSHIP CITY

ROMNEY, JARED LORENZO SUMMIT CO. WANSHIP CITY

SALISBURY, JAMES HENRY SUMMIT WANSHIP CITY

SMITH, CLARENCE SUMMIT CO. WANSHIP CITY

"Utah, Veterans with Federal Service Buried in Utah, Territorial to 1966," database with images, *FamilySearch* (https://familysearch.org/ark:/61903/1:1:FLRQ-7J7 : accessed 30 April 2016), Joshua H Bates, 04 Oct 1918; citing City Cemetery, France, military unit Co D 347 MG Bn 91 Div, Army, World War 1, State Archives, Capitol Building, Salt Lake City; FHL microfilm 485,498.

More information about Josh in these documents:

MACHINE GUN BATTALION 139

CASUALTIES OF THE 91st DIVISION.

MEUSE-ARGONNE OFFENSIVE, SEPTEMBER 26th-OCTOBER 12th, 1918

91st DIVISION	KILLED		WOUNDED SEVERELY		WOUNDED SLIGHTLY		GASSED		MISSING		PRIS-ONERS		TC	
	Off.	Men	Off.	Men	Off.	Men	Off.	Men	Off.	Men	Off.	Men	Off.	
Hq. of Division	1	1	1	5	3	1	1	1					6	8
346th M. G. Bn		3		2		6								11
181st Inf. Bg		1		1										2
348th M. G. Bn	2	27		19		92	1	2					3	140
347th M. G. Bn	3	35	9	39		88		18		4			12	184
361st Inf	7	275	10	231	19	625	1	34	1	16		2	38	1182
362nd Inf	12	210	15	398	14	436	8	104		18		6	49	1172
363rd Inf	5	155	8	129	15	498	8	79		26		1	36	888
364th Inf	6	124	21	344	4	270	5	96		33		1	36	868
316th Engineers	1	24	6	35	3	121	1	4		2			11	186
316th F. S. Bn		2	1	5	1	19		2					2	28
316th Trains		2		9	1	17	1						2	28
TOTAL	37	859	71	1217	60	2173	26	340	1	98		10	195	4697

YPRES-LYS OFFENSIVE, OCTOBER 29th-NOVEMBER 11th, 1918.

Division Hqs														
346th M. G. Bn				1		3		1						5
347th M. G. Bn		18		16		41		3						78
348th M. G. Bn		8		3	1	18							1	29
181st Inf. Bg														
361st Inf. Bg	3	37	5	31	3	77							11	145
362nd Inf	3	45	3	38	3	107	4	3					13	193
182nd Inf. Bg														
363d Inf	5	70	2	48	11	140		13				1	18	272
364th Inf	2	32	2	40	2	56		6		2			6	136
316th Engineers	1	4	1	5	2	11							4	20
316th F. S. Bn						2								2
316th Train		1	1	1		2		1					1	5
Sub-Total	14	215	14	183	22	457	4	27		2		1	54	885
53rd Art. Bg						1								1
107th F. Art		2		7		5				1				15
108th F. Art				13		2								15
109th F. Art		1	1	1		6		1		1			1	10
103rd Am. Tr		2		9		11		5						27
TOTALS	14	220	15	213	22	402	4	33		4		1	55	953
GRAND TOTAL	51	1079	86	1430	82	2655	30	373	1	102		11	250	5650

Calkins, J. Uberto. (1919). *History of the 347th machine gun battalion: Compiled from official records and the personal notes of various members of the battalion.* Oakland [Calif.]: Horwinsk

Number of 347th killed: ________

Number of 91st killed: ________

HISTORY OF THE 347th

OFFICIAL CIRCULATION ONLY)

Headquarters 91st Division A. E. F., January 29, 1919.

ORDERS:

No. 7.

1. The name "Wild West Division," by which this division has been known since the days of its organization at Camp Lewis, Washington, in 1917, is officially recognized as the distinctive divisional name.

2. The distinctive divisional design, a green fir tree, adopted as a personal badge, to be worn by each officer and man of the division (G. O. 57, 91st Division, 1918), is emblematic, not only of the foliage found in each state from which the personnel of this division was selected, but the evergreen and useful character of this foliage is emblematic also of the state of readiness and the degree of usefulness which has characterized, and should continue to be the aim of, each unit of the division.

3. Since this division was ready to participate in the St. Mihiel salient operation while standing in the reserve of the First American Army; since it was ready to attack in the front line of the Fifth Army Corps, from Forest de Hesse, when the Commander-in-Chief launched his attack against the enemy's line of communications between the Meuse River and the Argonne Forest; since some of its units were already entraining for Belgium before others, marching from the firing line, had reached the railroad; since its units never hesitated to attack the most formidable of the enemy's defenses in Belgium; and since its members are now ready, either to return to the United States and resume the pursuits of peace, or to continue their service wherever ordered by the Commander-in-Chief, the phrase "Always Ready" is adopted as the divisional motto.

BY COMMAND OF MAJOR GENERAL JOHNSTON.

OFFICIAL:
(D. J. COMAN)
Major, A. G.
Adjutant.

Henry C. Jewett,
Colonel, General Staff,
Chief of Staff.

GENERAL DISTRIBUTION.

(230—FOR OFFICIAL CIRCULATION ONLY)

Headquarters 91st Division A. E. F., February 24, 1919.

GENERAL ORDERS:

No. 16.

1. The following letter from the Commander-in-Chief, American Expeditionary Forces, generously commending this division for its participation in the campaign which led to the armistice, is published for the information of all officers and men of the division:

American Expeditionary Forces.
Office of the Commander-in-Chief.
France, February 20, 1919.

Name given to the 91st Division:

Divisional Design:

Meaning of the divisional design:

Insight: Josh and the Author

In chapters 3, 4, and 5 census records, family charts and family photographs acquainted you with Josh's parents and siblings. His parents had a moderately sized family for the times.

Joshua was 21 years old when his youngest sister was born in August 1916. She was so young, that she did not remember him. He left for training at Camp Lewis just after her second birthday. People are fortunate if they remember anything of significance at that age. Ruth Margaret did not. When he died she was three years old.

Ruth Margaret told me that the first memory she had regarding Joshua was his funeral in Utah when she was five. She remembers her mother crying. She remembers her older siblings being extremely sad. One of her specific memories is of the Army captain, who accompanied Josh's body, showing her card tricks at their dining room table.

Ruth Margaret was my mother. Joshua Henry Bates was my uncle. Remember that Rena married a Brinton? So did Ruth Margaret, a cousin of the man Rena married.

My Findings

Each chapter of sources about the life of Joshua Henry Bates includes a variety of primary, secondary and tertiary sources about his life which you read, interpreted, transcribed or summarized.

On the following pages are my answers to the chapter questions. You can compare your answers to mine.

- Will you discover the same facts I did?
- Will our interpretations or conclusions agree?
- Will you discover something that I overlooked?
  (Most readers do).

Chapter 1: The Suspect, My Findings

Joshua H. Bates was a striking young man. Not that his individual facial characteristics were notable by themselves, but he definitely was "decked out" for a studio portrait at Mr. Pearson's *Alseen Studio* in the center of Salt Lake City, only one block south of the historic and religious city center. He dressed in a tweed suit, dark tie and rounded collar dress shirt. His shiny hair was parted offset to the right of his forehead with waves sweeping backwards. His high forehead framed alert eyes under a strong brow. A tan from his nose down indicated that he worked outside while wearing a hat. Even though his ears were prominent, they were proportionate with his straight, long nose and full mouth and oval chin. His bright eyes and slight smile made me think that he is hiding a humorous secret (Joshua H. Bates). The distinctive rounded collar is a "club collar," popular in the early 20th century when the club, or rounded Eaton, collars were a mainstay of a man's wardrobe (Hugh & Crye).

I found an encyclopedia illustration of a man in 1916 with a collar and jacket that was similar to Joshua's (Wikipedia). He was dressed with a rounded collar and a suit jacket with lapels staggered in size, smallest point attached to the jacket collar while the lower lapel was wider and larger, just like Joshua's.

Men's styles change slowly compared to women. Hair is no different. The Edwardian offset part and waves continues in fashion for young men well into the Progressive Era.

The back of the photograph records "Joshua Bates." There is no date.

Chapter 2: Starting at the End, My Findings

What did you discover in the obituary? Let's see if my list of facts from the obituary includes what you found. Star each fact if you also discovered the same.

1. Title showed the article is from Summit County.
2. Title declared that he died for world liberty.
3. Location of news article was "Wanship, Summit Co., Nov 29." No year is given.
4. Parents were Mr. and Mrs. Joshua Bates.
5. Parents received notice of his death via a telegram from the War Department.
6. Joshua H. Bates was a private.
7. He went to Camp Lewis in September 1917.
8. He received training at Camp Lewis.
9. He was a member of the 347th Machine Gun Battalion.
10. He landed in France on July 22, 1918.
11. The telegram said that he was killed on October 4, 1918 while operating his machine gun.
12. Joshua H. Bates was a native of Wanship.
13. He was 23 years of age.
14. He was a graduate of North Summit high school.
15. He studied 2 summers at University of Utah.
16. He was the principal of Wanship School for two years.
17. He lefta father, mother, 3 brothers and 2 sisters.

If you did not find an item that I listed, it may have been the information from the headline? Do not overlook headlines. They should contain at least a kernel or two of fact.

Chapter 3: Everyone Has a Family-the U.S. Census, My Findings

The 1900 Census:

The Joshua Bates family census was enumerated on June 13, 1900 in Wanship, Summit, Utah by Charles H. West. The digitized image shows the original document as Supervisor's District No. 273, Enumeration No. 138, page 6 of the *Twelfth Census of the United States*. The dwelling number was 102 and the family number was 106. Enumerators asked the same questions at every household.

Joshua Bates was the head of the household, white, male and born in Apr 1869. At the time of the census he was 31 years old and married for six years. He was born in Utah but his mother and father were both born in England. He owned his home with no mortgage and had a farm. He was as a sheepherder and he was not unemployed for any month of the previous year. He could read, write and had attended school.

Eliza (the squiggle indicates a same last name of Bates) was his wife, white, female and born in November 1872 in Utah. At the time of the census she was 27 years old and married for six years, having given birth to their two sons, both living. Her father was born in Denmark and her mother in Germany. No occupation was listed. She attended school and could read and write.

Joshua H. Bates was the elder son, born Apr 1895 in Utah. At census time he was a five-year-old white male and single. He had no formal schooling to date.

Andrew P. Bates was the younger son, born July 1898 and was one-year-old.. He was a white, single male with no formal schooling to date.

The 1910 Census:

By the 1910 census, some questions of the census and the family had changed quite a bit. The Supervisor's District No. was 1 Utah, Enumeration No. 167, sheet 3B, and the Bates were family number 49. The enumerator, George L. Hobson, visited on April 27,1910. The dwelling number was 46 and the family number was 49.

Joshua Bates was still the head of the family, white, male and born in 1869. He was 41 years old and had been married for 15 years, and a notation of "M1" in the marriage column indicated that this was a first marriage. He spoke English, and his parents were both born in England, but Joshua was born in Utah. He was listed as a farmer and an employer. He still owned his own home and farm with no mortgage on either one. His farm was on farm schedule 33. Joshua could read and write, but he did not attend school in the current school year. He was not a veteran. He was not blind or deaf.

Eliza Bates was now 37 and a mother of four living children of four births. Profession was marked as "none." She spoke English and was born in Utah. Her father was born in Denmark and her mother in Germany. She could read and write.

Joshua H. Bates was 15 years old and Andrew P. Bates was 11. New additions, since the 1900 census, to the family were a boy, Roy R. Bates, age 7 and a daughter, Dorothy M., age 2. All the boys attended school since September 1,1899 and were hired as farm workers by their father.

~~~~~~~~~~~~

Have you found other information that I have not found? Sometimes seasoned researchers skip over items that are thought to be common knowledge.

Though the data is informative, census records lack a sensitivity of a personal life story. Nonetheless, I could now write a family narrative based on the information discovered in these censuses. Not only that, I have discovered the countries of origin of Joshua H. Bates grandparents. What reason would persons from England, Denmark and Germany have for leaving their home countries in the 1860s?

Chapter 4: Reading Family Data Charts, My Findings

The Joshua Henry Bates family chart added the complete family structure to his life's vital information. Actually, this particular chart showed the family for his parents, Joshua and Eliza Petersen Bates, that included Joshua Henry and his six siblings. His parents were Joshua and Eliza (Petersen) Bates who were both born in Wanship, Summit County, Utah. Joshua was three years older than his wife. They lived their entire lives in Wanship. All seven children were born in Wanship over a course of 19 years. Eliza died in Wanship in 1946. At some point Joshua moved to Vancouver, Clark County, Washington where he died. One or more of his children moved there. He died when he was 89 years old.

Joshua Henry Bates was their first child. He was born April 2, 1895. The entire row of information for him showed no marriage date as with five other brothers and sisters. The abbreviation "UNMD," written in the marriage spaces, probably stood for unmarried. He was so young when he died in October 4, 1918, that he could have been unmarried. This family data chart also showed his middle name: Henry. All we knew before this chart was his middle initial.

The family had three more brothers. I could tell that because of the name choices. Who would name a girl Parley? There was also a column before the name column that said "SEX M F" and either M or F was written in front of the name. I noticed two irregularities with two sisters. Dorothy Marie died just after her third birthday. I remember seeing her photograph in an earlier chapter. How sad for her parents. She was a cute little girl. Then Effie Lucille died when she was only 35 years old! I wonder if it was an accident or some horrible disease like cancer or tuberculosis. The third girl, Ruth Margaret, lived a long time. She married twice. She died on Christmas day at 93 years of age.

This record is a primary source. The reason is that Andrew PARLEY Bates wrote down the information and he appears on the chart as the second son. He should have know the information well, being an elder son of Joshua and Eliza.

Chapter 5: Everyone Has a Family: Photographs, My Findings

1. The Family Photograph

The persons in this studio family photograph are: Back row from the left, Andrew Parley, Joshua Henry and Roy Richard. Front row from the left, Joshua Bates, father; Effie Lucille, Lorenzo John, Ruth Margaret, Eliza Bates, mother. There is no studio identification on this photograph as it is a poor copy of the photograph, passed down to relatives.
~~~~~~~~~~~~

The problem:

The "family group sheet" of the Bates in the last chapter listed seven children. In this family photograph there are only six, two teen boys, one young man and three little ones, a girl, a boy and a baby girl. Dorothy Marie is missing. She was born in 1907 after Roy Richard in 1903. The same record shows that she died in 1910. So, it makes sense that she is not in this photograph taken after August 1916 when Ruth Margaret was born, and Ruth appears to be around a year old in this photograph. So, I estimate the photograph to be taken in June through August in 1917, a little over a month from when Joshua left for Camp Lewis, and a year and three to four months before Joshua's death.

2. Three Children Photograph

The next photograph is of three children taken in a studio by W. E. Lewis. After reading about cabinet card photographs, I would bet that the original was one. The boys appear to be related. The two boys have the same part in their hair and all three have similar eyes. It is a studio shot rather than an exterior shot or in home. The background, including the plant, are paintings. As I compare the faces to the last photograph I am struck by how I can identify Joshua Henry and Andrew Parley right away. It has to be a special occasion. Both older boys are wearing boutonnieres in their suit jackets. But the next in birth order is Roy Richard, not a little girl. I lucked out because the names are written on the back of the photograph. It is Roy Richard, in a dress, with a girly hairstyle. At least his stockings and shoes look like boy's. I would not have accurately guessed their ages of 8, 11 and 3, without the light age notations behind their names on the back of the photograph. I found a website, *Historic Boy Clothing,* that discusses boy clothing evolutions. Little boys did have curly hairdos! They wore large bow ties. It was a rite of passage for the mother to take the little son to the photographer for a photograph before and after the curls were wacked off. The mothers often cried as they realized that the little toddler would now identify more with his father, and in Roy's case, older brothers. Many mothers would then go back to the photographer studio for a "post-cut" photograph. Perhaps the Bates family could not afford two, but that is just an assumption. I hope this was also the time when he could graduate to knickers like his brother Parley wore. All little kids love growing up, and as the article pointed out, many would eagerly look forward to the scissors. I bet some were not so excited about it as they saw it as a separation from their doting moms. It is interesting that few little boys have as elaborate a rite of passage these days. I know that many parents photograph their children's first haircuts, save a lock, and sometimes pay double because the toddler boy is so much to handle for the barber. Anyway, my husband says that is what his parents faced.

3. Toddler boy photograph

The third studio photograph of the dapper toddler boy must be Joshua Henry. He is wearing the oversized bowtie, a flouncy shirt, a discreetly masculine skirt, and boots. I have a theory that Mrs. Bates had a post-haircut photography session for Joshua. His hair is coiffed so exactly, with a little forehead wave. Building on my theory, I think that the last photograph was on Roy Richard's first haircut day at age three, I am assuming that this is Joshua Henry's third birthday also.

The photograph also supports the common knowledge that the first child, the sole planet orbiting the mother, garners more attention and expenses. His clothing indicates her attention to him, while in the previous photograph, Roy Richard is not so masculine in his gingham dress. Poor Roy.

A cabinet card is a photograph on a heavy card, with a specific size, that was popular in the late 1800s, useful for dating photography. It is about 4 x 6 inches in size and its names comes from being suitable to display in cabinets. The two examples here have the photographer's name written or embossed on the bottom of the card. Joshua Henry's photograph has "Ellis & Goodwin, 64 West, Second South St. Salt Lake City" embossed on the bottom margin. (Cabinet Card Web Article).

According to the article on labeling photographs a person should label all photographs with full names and ages and location in soft-lead pencil. Often other pen or gel or felt tip options dent the photograph or leach through the back to the photograph.

The chart records that each photograph had a different background. I wish we had an original of the entire family's photograph. Because of its orientation, I do not know that it is a cabinet card. The examples I found were only produced in a portrait orientation. I am not sure there is enough room for the photographer information in the landscape view. But this is an assumption.

Since we are lucky enough to pinpoint the years of these photographs, 1917, 1910 and 1888, the dress can be used for examples of country folks' best dress in turn-of-the-century Utah. I think the best photograph is of Joshua Henry at age three. The composition is pleasing, with posed arms and legs. The props and Joshua divide the photograph into proper thirds. The photograph of the three boys is nice, but the throw on the floor does not cover the entire bottom of the scene. The boys are not posed creatively. It could have been improved by inching Roy Richard toward Joshua Henry, with Joshua having a brotherly arm around the little guy. But Roy Richard looks a little grumpy and he may have wished to be even farther away from his brothers. I imagine that the second photographer was less expensive than the one for Joshua, as his name was written rather than embossed on the cabinet card The family shot is a formally arranged, balanced photograph, with the photographer trying to get all subjects with their eyes open, looking at the camera, and not moving any body parts. The photographer did an admirable job.

Chapter 6: Analyzing Other Photos, My Findings

The first thing I noticed was the little girl with the arm akimbo and a smile. Next, I could not miss that this is an impromptu posed shot, probably at home in Wanship, Utah with the children in their everyday clothing, even with requisite dirt. Unlike formal photography, three of the four children are smiling or laughing, and the photograph is outside with no need for those scary popping flashbulbs of the day. I even remember that in the early 1950s itinerate photographs took photographs of me at our family service station and motel on the old Route 99 that is now Interstate 5 in Washington State. He made prints and attached one to a calendar for my mother. I was in saddle shoes, cord pants and a plaid jacket that my mother had sewn. I wish I still had that jacket as my mother discontinued sewing soon after that.

From the left, we see Andrew Parley amused by his little sister Dorothy Marie. Next is Joshua Henry in his overalls, giving us a pursed mouth smile. On the right is Roy Richard, still not too amused by photography. In the window behind them a decorative horse is displayed. I wonder if it is wooden and a Scandinavian painted horses?

The house had clapboard siding and due to the photograph being black and white, I cannot tell if it was painted a dark color or weathered wood. The window was a sash window, opened by pulling up the bottom pane. There did not appear to be any grass but perhaps dirt and rocks.

Andrew Parley was taking such delight in Dorothy Marie in the photograph. She looked about three years old. Her birthday was in July 1910. Could this be a photographic memory of that day? Andrew Parley looked about 10, Joshua Henry looked perhaps 14 and Roy Richard looked about 7 or 8. Though my estimates are a little off from the data in their family record in chapter two, I am sticking with the late spring or summer of 1910 as Marie (she was called by her middle name) looks like a three-year-old. Marie died just after her 3rd birthday, August 28, 1910. Poor parents! This was probably Marie's last photograph.

I wonder if the family has more photographs of Marie? Was Joshua Henry a "hayseed" as he appears? He looks like a goofball, nothing bad intended, but I think he probably had a goofy sense of humor. Andrew Parley looks like a fun kid, as does Marie. Roy....my jury is still out about him.

My Title:
Playtime Break
My Caption:
Eliza and Joshua's kids take a time from chores and play for a photograph at home.
My Summary:
Photographed were, from the left, Andrew Parley, Dorothy Marie, Joshua Henry and Roy Richard Bates, the four children of Joshua and Eliza Petersen Bates of Wanship, Utah. An itinerate photographer snapped the impromptu photograph as he visited homes in the area. The Utah Division of State History, http://utsl.sirsi.net, has a collection of itinerate photographer information, but there was no information recorded for this photograph when I searched for "Wanship, Utah."

Chapter 7: Records of Josh's Youth, My Findings

I imagine that few records for children are found, especially at Joshua's time, as slates were used in school and few assignments could be shared with parents. It is probably presumptuous to assume that parents of the time did not care to save their children's toys and creations.

If it is important to keep items, assignments or writings for our ancestors, we had better identify the items' creator and organize them so that we establish that it was important to us. I want to preserve my writings, my talks, articles I have written, items I created, or at least a photograph of the item from all sides. I would want to save my Maleficent costume that I sewed and wore often on Halloween, entertaining the teenagers of my high school. My journals are really neglected, but they are pretty thorough when I did write in them. My collections reveal much about me. Probably just photographs would be better than someone having to deal with all the collections.

The newspaper article announced the eighth grade graduation commencement of Summit County schools. It was a rite of passage as many finished their education at eighth grade. Joshua was the only graduate from Wanship District No. 4.

Family records might include birth certificates, photographs, report cards, art work, textile handiwork, journals, letters, newspaper articles, talks, essays, pretty much what my parents or I would save.

Church records could include birth announcements, blessing or confirmation certificates, baptismal records, special awards or commendations, and certificates of advancement in youth programs.

School records could include essays written, art created, report cards, programs for graduation, school class photographs, play programs, or sports awards.

Josh's first report card called a "Summit Stake Academy Registration Card" showed his classes and also his grades in Theology, English, Algebra and Physiography. He received straight As on October 30, 1911. The next year his October 8, 1912 report card showed many more classes: Theology, English, Math, History, Drawing, Manual T which was perhaps a vocational class. His grades were listed in numerical marks, respectively of 92, 93, 92, 95, 80 and 92. Drawing was his only B-, if the scale of scores is like today.

The next record was a church record, but it had no title. It listed his name as Joshua H. Bates, born in Wanship, Utah on April 2, 1895. His parents were Joshua Bates and Eliza Petersen. He was blessed on June 6, 1895 by Ebenezer R. Young. Joshua was baptized on August 15, 1903 by Frank D Hixson, and confirmed the next day, August 16, 1903 by Henry Reynolds. Josh was ordained a deacon on February 3, 1908 by William [Wm] Crook. He was ordained a teacher on February 12, 1912 by Alma Gibbons. The front had no title, but was a record of his ordination as an elder on November 26, 1916 in Wanship, Utah.

A great school photograph of the entire school in Wanship, followed with a few extra toddlers included on the right side of the front row. The Bates kids were pretty easily identified. Joshua was wearing his overalls from the photograph in chapter six. Parley looked like a mini Joshua, complete with overalls in the center row. Roy was in the front row, still not looking particularly impressed. There was no label on the photograph and it was only a photocopy. I do not know if the school shot photographs in the spring or in the fall. But I can tell that it was the old rock school built in 1866. A new red brick school house with two classrooms was in service by the fall of 1912. If this really was Marie as I theorize, this photograph was probably taken either the fall of 1909 or the spring of 1910. (Summit County website, "Wanship Church and School" page).

Josh's registration card for Oct 13, 1914 listed a huge number of classes: English, American History, Rural Economics, Oral Exposition, Music, Civics, Physiology, and Elementary Algebra. He pulled straight As again, except for a B+ in music. It appeared that he did well in music and drawing, but not well enough to keep company with the rest of his As.

Joshua graduated from North Summit High School on May 27, 1915. He was twenty-one years old. I am not positive as to why he graduated later than our normal 18 years of age. He wasn't a slacker. My suspicion is that he was important to the agricultural success of his father. Seeds needed sowing and tending, then they were harvested. Caring for livestock had cyclical responsibilities also. People did not buy food, but grew and raised it. It was the priority to sustain life. There was also the possibility that they started school later than we do today, with fewer classes per year. That said, Joshua was the valedictorian of the class, delivering the valedictory speech. There were eleven in the graduating class.

Chapter 8: Joshua's Journal Begins, My Findings

TRANSCRIPTION:

Journal of
Joshua H. Bates
Wanship, Utah
Born April 2, 1895
Diary begun April 2, 1916

Please yourself and do our duty as you see it.
Act natural, be yourself.
When you do a thing make it go.
Pleasure is not all there is in life but enjoy yourself.
When your chance comes take it, it soon passes probably never to return.
Do not talk to hear your own voice when speaking have a purpose and make your *you (crossed out)* words as few as will convey the meaning.

It was Joshua's 21st birthday. That is momentous for anyone. Based on the preamble to his journal that I transcribed, Joshua seemed to be outlining his personal guidelines for his young adult years.

Joshua may have created this list of advice because he struggled with each. Or he could have created the list based on what he really believed or did. From what I know thus far, I believe that he did his duty and that he finished anything that he started. He probably needed the advice to enjoy himself as he was so duty-bound. He wanted to take advantage of opportunities as they came. He seemed to worry about letting go and enjoying himself, and about talking too much, perhaps nervous talking?

Chapter 9: University Days, My Findings

1. Mon. June 12
   Up to the University and register for Summer School in the forenoon in the afternoon I go out to Uncle Fred's place to a couple of shows at night with Everett.

2. Thursday June 15
   To school all day home and out to dance at Saltair at night a good time home & to-bed by 12:00.

3. Friday June 16.
   To school. The faculty give the Summer Students a reception in the afternoon. Rather a formal affair not a very good time. Home at 5:30 in at night.

4. Monday June 19 To school all day
   Tues. 20 To school all day home at night
   Wednesday June 21 To school al day home at night

Thursday School all day

Friday June 23 To school all day. To picture show at night.

Educational Certificates:

A. Teacher Examination Grades	July 15, 1915	Grades
B. University of Utah fee	Jan 8, 1916	Correspondence class fee
C. University of Utah receipt	Jun 12, 1916	Summer school receipt
D. University of Utah fee	Dec 7, 1916	University registration fee
E. University of Utah fee	Dec 22, 1916	Manual fee
F. County Teacher's Certificate	August 3, 1916	Can teach elementary school in Utah
G. Grammar Grade County Teacher's Certificate	August 14, 1916	Attests to good moral character & passed tests on subjects to teach
H. Utah Education Association	December 20, 1916	Payment of dues to the UEA

Chapter 10: On the Town, My Findings

1916, page 16

Thursday, June 15: To school at University of Utah,
To Dance at Saltair

Friday, June 16: To school at University of Utah, Reception by faculty for students

Saturday, June 17: To Salt Lake Theatre with Edd Young to see "Birth of a Nation"
To Majestic Park with Edd Young to a dance
To uptown Salt Lake City with Edd Young to a café

Sunday, June 18: Home all day, read, slept, loaf, study, write

1916, page 17

Thursday, June 29: To school at University of Utah

Friday, June 30: To school at University of Utah
To Saltair, Mr. Sharp and lady friends, good time

Saturday, July 1: Home all day
Visit Clara
Dance at night

Sunday, July 2: Home all day, reading "Lepord [leopard?] Spots"
Visited by Ruth and Lisle

Monday, July 3: Home, read until noon
Home, visited with Uncle Fred's folks

Tuesday, July 4: Home until 3:30 PM
Downtown, picture show
Home, supper
7:15PM train for Saltair, met Vinnie Rigby and Miss Kirk and other girls

1916, Page 18

Tuesday, July 4: Saltair, Everett arrives, won't dance, leaves
Saltair, multiple girls, dances until they leave
Saltair, more girls mentioned by name, cuts in to dance

	Saltair, "such a crowd," extra train at 2:00 AM
	Depot to home, 6th Avenue car
Wednesday, July 5:	Late to school at University of Utah
	Home, napped until supper
	Home, studied
Thursday, July 6:	To school at University of Utah
	Home, studied
Friday, July 7:	To school at University of Utah
	Home, afternoon
	Humorous picture show

Chapter 11: Sweet on Someone, My Findings

Considering the directions for this chapter, I assume that Rena and Josh were the subjects of the photograph on the first page of Chapter 11, page 15. She was dressed is a light colored, maybe white, dress that looked very comfortable for hot and dry Utah summers. Josh was in a suit and a flat-top hat., perhaps a straw hat. The background was interesting. The photograph had to be in Utah due to the mountains in the distance, but directly behind them was a palm tree. There appeared to be train tracks in the lower half of the photo.

In his journal Josh mentioned that on the Fourth of July he went to downtown Salt Lake City to a movie or as he said, a "picture show." It just occurred to me that "picture show" was the accurate term of the time. And since there were no "talkies" until about 1929 he would not have used the term "silent film" as he would not have distinguished "picture shows" of his time were anything but silent.

Josh went home for supper then hopped a 7:15 PM train to Saltair. Saltair! That explains the tracks and the palm tree. It was the playground destination for bathing and dancing in the Salt Lake Valley. He mentioned that there was a huge crowd, I assume due to it being Independence Day. It is interesting that during both years of the journal he never mentioned the holiday. Anyway, he met Vinnie Rigby and Miss Kirk and some other girls there with whom they visited. On page 16 of the journal, he continued by mentioning that Everett came but did not dance and left on the early train. But Josh danced with girls until they left. Then he resorted to cutting in on other couples so that he could dance more. He listed various young women dancers: Miss Claig, Miss Montgomery, Miss Leeman, Miss Christenson, Miss De Young and more. There was such a large crowd that the commuter trains back to the city did not hold everyone. He waited for "the extra" that left Saltair at 2:00 AM. Luckily the street car company still had a line at the depot and he was able to take the Sixth Avenue car, making it home in bed by 2:30 AM. He must have a swell time as he ends his journal entry mentioning it again.

Josh seemed like a fun-loving guy. He enjoyed being in big Salt Lake City for his University of Utah studies and a bevy of entertainment at night. He loved dancing. Closing down the house was okay with him and he was lucky the street cars were still running as Salt Lake City blocks are about four times longer than Washington city blocks.

I cannot help but wonder how classes went for him and fellow partiers the next day at his University of Utah classes.

Monday July 10, 1916 he was in class all day, then went home to press his clothes for a run down to Rigby's after supper, to take Rena to a show. (Interesting, that a Wanship girl appeared to lodge in Salt Lake City for the summer also. I am not sure if she was studying at the University of

Utah or somewhere else, or spending the summer with relatives). The couple nixed the movie plans to walk to the Kirks to spend the evening with Dorus and "his girl". Josh and Rena took a little walk and he delivered her back to Rigby's.

Later on July 22nd Josh and Rena were still dating. I had to laugh at this entry because if he and Parley had cell phones to text one another, they could have found each other without Josh trailing Parley around town. Discovering that Parley had gone to a show with Pearl and Clara, Josh, Rena, Miss Nelson and Bert attended a show called *Where Are My Children*. He mentioned that it was "a good moral play." There is a good summary of the plot on *Wikipedia: (https://en.wikipedia.org/wiki/Where_Are_My_Children%3F)*. IMBd mentioned that the film was banned at the time as being immoral (http://www.imdb.com/title/tt0007558). I am rather surprised that abortion was a subject of a movie in 1916, that the subject would raise itself from the shadows.

The following day, Sunday July 23, 1916, the "bunch" (Rena, Parley, Fred, Everett, Vinnie, Edith, Bert, and Sid) had another day of fun. They attended a show, then went to the Palace for ice cream. Josh took Rena back to Kirks at night. Now I am really confused as to where she stayed. He slept at Uncle Fred's.

On Monday the guys went get the girls and they were off again to Saltair. They went "bathing" in the lake, and danced at night.

By Saturday Josh and Parley were at the family farm in Wanship, working on a ditch in the morning and turning hay in the afternoon. But true to form, they had time to go to a show in Coalville that evening. Parley drove Josh and Rena who sat in the back seat. Josh was rather cryptic, but he mentioned that the evening had a "souvenir." Sunday morning Josh was a bit under the weather, no surprise, considering the partying all week, laying around until 3:00PM. He spent the evening with...Rena.

A few weeks later on August 13, 1916, he mentioned that a few things are "cleared up" and that he hoped to have everything resolved by the end of the week. His talk of forewarning and preventative steps sounded ominous. Did something happen between him and Rena?

It appeared that he was not just on a break from University of Utah, but off for the rest of the summer. So haying and working for others in August took up his time. On August 18th he was off to a dance at Coalville after haying. He mentioned that music was provided by a group from Park City, that he had a "swell" time and that Miss Cohen was one of the best dancers. By August 30th he had singing practice, afterward visiting Rena. No dance.

There wasn't much romance information all fall, but Josh was really busy teaching. Finally, on Christmas day he had "a little conflab" at Rena's home "with no anger on [his] part". It must have worked out as Rena, Sid and Joshua were on a train for Park City by late afternoon.

By January 1917 Josh was back teaching at school. On January 30th he visited Rena while she tended a neighbor's home. He wrote that it was 'an eventful night," underlined. He was so cryptic that is hard to say what made it eventful. I wonder if he was worried that little siblings would read his journal.

The next day, he missed school for the first time in his career. He sat around his Aunt Mary's for a while then headed home. Mother Bates informed him that he has contracted the measles and sent him to bed. Rena came over. The next day he felt badly, but had few breakouts. Rena came over. By Friday he described himself as "Some Looker" with red chafing all over his face. Rena came over. The next day he spent all day in bed. Rena came over.

On February 4 he was still sick. This was the first time he wrote about the war with Germany. He hoped that nothing would come of it. Rena came over. This time he mentioned that they talked quite a while. On Monday, February 5th he arose for a few hours but was really shaky. Rena came over. Tuesday he was up all day. Rena came over. On Wednesday he was around home all day and wanted to read, but could not. He was exasperated. On Thursday Sid came to play checkers and Josh actually went outside for about five minutes. Rena came over at night. On Friday Josh went "on the lam" to Smiths' house, then to Homer's. Rena came over at night.

By Saturday Josh was able to read some of *The Right of the Strongest* which is now called an important historical work, according to an abstract on Amazon.com. He walked to Aunt Mary's, then Smiths. Arriving home, he discovered that his littlest brother, Ren, had contracted the measles.

By Sunday Josh was feeling pretty good. He pressed his clothes, tidied his rooms and wrote in his journal before dinner. In the evening he walked to Homer's and then over to Rena's to return home at midnight, welcomed by a lecture. He must have felt better if his parents, one or the other or both, lectured him for doing too much. One observation about Rena: I think she had the Florence Nightingale syndrome. She really went overboard to see him every day.

By the next month Joshua was in full swing. On Sunday March 4 he attended to Sunday School, meeting and Mutual. After Mutual he said that he did something unexpected, he went to Homer's. Apparently he was to have gone to Rena's as he reported that she was "some-what peeved." He taught school the next day and then went to Rena's at night, brave man! They practiced the play and he said that he still wondered about their relationship.

On Saturday March 10th he farmed with his brother Parley and his father in the morning, then attended a principal meeting in Coalville in the afternoon. He had a shave and haircut while there and went home to practice at night. Literally, between the lines, he wrote that "things look brighter." He was up late.

The next Friday night, school was dismissed early for a church reunion. He was a typical young guy at potluck dinners, eating "until I nearly burst." He waddled home to get ready for a dance that night. He didn't have a good time, admitting that he "twisted things up a bit." Not only was he up until 2:00 AM that night, but the next night he also practiced late. The problem was not mentioned, of course; but he was nervous about doing the right thing. The nerves were a setup for failure.

The following Thursday he worked all day at school and made penance to Rena by washing dishes with her. They had a play meeting and discussion. It sounded like Rena and he kept hashing over the same issues, not knowing what they were going to do. He went home and wrote a poem called "You Do Not Care." He went to work all day and called Rena in and read the poem to her. He said that he didn't know what to think. I did not read the poem, but with a title like that he was lucky that he was still alive.

It seemed that he felt out of control of his life. To achieve some autonomy and to start fresh, he applied for a new teaching position at Hoytsville School.

The next night he drove to Hoytsville with Sid and Rena. He mentioned that he had to swallow something quite difficult, but that he did not regret it as the situation turned out pretty well before the night was over.

By his twenty-second birthday Josh and Rena's relationship was still good. Rena came to his house, he took her home, washed some more dishes and received a birthday present. Josh mentioned that a third of his life was over! That's only 66 years of age. Most men in 1918 lived even a shorter amount of time. Above the birthday entry he wrote, "Evidence is lacking. Yet I still hope," which I thought so provocative that I made those sentences this book's title.

Josh was pretty hard on himself. A month after his 22nd birthday he was still berating himself for being an idiot. I wonder when he began to feel that way? I felt the relationship with Rena was just too hard to maintain and frankly, I became bored with it. Later in May he took her to a small social. I guess love is blind as he still hoped, and said that the "plot thickens." Yet a week later, he said that he blundered again.

On June 3, 1917 he wondered about a tidbit of information that he heard about Rena. The poor guy. In a few weeks, after working on a road in the canyon, he decided to go to a dance in Coalville by himself.

By July 15th not only was ice cream cold, but so was his reception. So, he spent the evening with Miss Nelson. The next night he visited Miss Nelson again and received a cold reception from her. Then a few days later on Wednesday, July 18th, some warming happened at the Smith home. Nonetheless, relations were still on the cool side as he and Everett saw Rena and Edith while at Saltair on July 24th, rather than taking her. By the next night, they were enjoying themselves on the town. All seemed to go well. Well, maybe not. We know that other things were happening in August 1917 that affected this star-crossed couple.

Chapter 12: Josh the Poet, My Findings

Mother.

Your princely halls and wealth untold
Can never equal in pure gold,
The love of a mother for her son.
Measured not in pounds, nor yet by ton,
But by the acts of loving grace,
That makes to him his mother's face
Dearer far than fame or power;
For to him she is the lofty tower
Of hope, of prayers, and love untold,
The one, who when young or growing old,
Is doing acts of her own free will
To ease our burdens or lift them, until
No matter how we love, father, sister, brother
None is so dear as our angle [angel] mother.

Analysis of the Writing

1. This writing is a poem.
2. The subject is his mother, Eliza Petersen Bates.
3. Her love for a son, her hope, her prayers, choosing to ease burdens to lift the burdens totally
4. Josh loves his mother more than any other family member. He loves seeing her face more than fame or power. Her love cannot be measured by any amount of wealth. Seeing her as a "lofty tower" shows how much he looks up to her. He admires that she has always helped others, even taking on their burdens, of her own free will.
5. Princely halls in line 1looks like frinaly hulls." Grace at the end of line 5 looks like "yrau." Power at the end of like 7 looks like "ferver." The problem is that the d, p, and a have loosely written loops that make the words confusing.
6. I wonder if he wrote this poem at a later date, since it is not dated.

Chapter 13: All in a Day's Work, My Findings

Transcriptions of journal excerpts:

1. 1916 Fri Apr. 21 — Up in time to catch the morning train to Coalville to give Eighth Grade Examination. Leave school building about 4:00 and go up to supper. After Supper Parley &
2. Saturday April 22 — Conduct Examinations in fore-noon After dinner I help other principals correct papers. Only one of my Eighth grade Students got through. To the show at night. To bed at Mrs. Powells at 11:00.
3. Monday April 24 — To school all day. To show at night Walters Company presented "Sowing the Winds," A good play presented by a good cast of characters. An English play of the upper class of society. Showing vice and corruptions of some of that class. To bed at 11:30.
4. Tuesday April 25 — To school all day. To show at night Walters Company presented "Corianton," by Prestus U. Bean: A Book of Mormon play of rare quality. To bed at 11:15
5. Wednesday May 10 — To school all day. Down to meeting at night preparing for pro gram at Homecoming of Oley Petersen. (Joshua has repaired auto mobiles, built roads, mined for copper, builds a nice secretary desk, wrote plays, sang in groups. He was pretty talented in many ways).
6. Friday May 12 — To school and checked up books and gave short program in fore noon. Gave the children a dance in the afternoon. Home and to bed early.
7. Wednesday May 24 — we are going to plant potatoe's in until 3:00. Then I come home and get ready to go to Coalville to the annual North Summit High School Banquet. Have a good time home and to bed at 12-45. In margin: "Adair" sung Miss Hobson.
8. Tuesday Sep 12 — To school all day. Start Recitations to day Students as usual not very bright after a long rest. Home at night write three letters one to R. and to-bed 10:15.
9. Thursday Nov 16 — To school all day. Have arithmetic nearly all day. The students are very dense or else I could not get it over to them.

10. Sat Dec 16	To school all day. To program in Hall at night. School gives program.
11. Mon Jan 1 1917	To children's dance in afternoon and get an invitation to dinner over to Smiths. A good spread. We decide to stay in Wanship for the Dance at night if there is a good crowd but if not we will leave for Coalville after the Game of Basket Ball. A fair crowd so we dance In Wanship. Home at 9:45.
12. Friday Mar 23	To school all day. Home down to hall over to store and school house. Call Rena in and read poem. I don't know what to think spend evening in playing singing reading and writing. Make application for Holtsville school for 1917-1918. Will hear from it in a few days
13. Sat Apr 17	To Coalville in morning on train to get a hair cut and see Mr. Neeley about school teaching at Echo. Down to Sims with May Pinio in afternoon Eat supper at hotel. Call up Rena.
13. Tuesday May 1	To school all day Supt. Kearns comes in for awhile in the morning and says nothing as usual. At night I take Parley to
14. Wednesday May 16	To school all day. Make out reports at night after school. Over to Hixsons at night to practice song with Miss Sinkins. Charles Horton takes us for a ride. Home 12:!0. To nights performance makes a stir.
15. Thursday May 17	To school all day. We have a small social at night R. decides to go with me. Small program and games and
16. Thursday Sept 6	Catch train to Coalville for teachers institute. Attend meetings in morning and afternoon. Home 5.25 Father mother Rena & I go to Coalville to a show
17. Friday Sept 7	To Coalville in car shave to meetings and then go to Echo to find a boarding place. Can find nothing under $30 per mo. Home, on way picking up Floss Mabel and Irene rec. Take Rena to the dance given by Park City Orchestra a good time. <u>Discussion</u>
18. Saturday Sept 8	To farm and mow. Afternoon until I break out the tongue from machine. To Smiths Saturday night, music, etc..
19. Sunday Sept 9	Do not go…[covered with Echo Canyon School photograph]
20. Monday Sept 10	Open up school. Talk with Miss Mighn a while, then home. Write letter to Rena To-bed

Chapter 14: Josh on Josh, My Findings

Three activities that stood out were that he prospected for copper, built roads and loved to dance.

The entry for April 18,1916 made me smile. He wouldn't have minded making lots of money, but in the meantime, he had papers to correct.

The next entries from April 26 through April 28th again showed all the activities he was involved with: buying coal (and probably shoveling it), journal writing, going for rides with friends, building a garage foundation, mixing cement. He made an interesting entry about dressing for church and then backing out. That had never been an issue for him before. He had even spoken at church many times.

On December 23rd he mentioned shopping, and when Everett could not go to town with him, he traveled to town alone for a "little rampage," whatever that means. He seemed to be a pretty nice guy....probably he had a double scoop of ice cream.

In March he wondered about "what he is good for" and what would make him happy. He said that he vacillated between taking charge and feeling low. He wondered if he had been dealt a raw deal. He wanted to develop a plan, have an anchor in life, but just did not know what he really wanted. In April he was still lecturing himself, and wrote that he needed to give himself a good "kick along" now and then. Later that Sunday he taught a lesson on "True to Oneself" and felt like no one was impressed. By the end of April he was so depressed that he was totally confused, could not study, could not get out of bed early without excruciating effort. He knew that he felt better six months ago, and was determined to get his strength back. The next day he and his brother Parley had a great time singing and playing the piano. I feel that he was improving. I wonder if it was situational depression.

The next excerpts were from August 1917 with a big heading at the top of the page saying "Evidence is lacking. Yet I still hope." And it's underlined. He is so obscure it is doubtful to what he is referring: his new job, Rena, the war? He took a day-long teachers examination and had a good time going to a show that night. On Friday he had more exams in the 'forenoon." In the afternoon he reported to the sheriff's office for a military physical. He made no comment about it. But the next two days he spent much time visiting friends, going to dances and hearing a player piano.

Chapter 15: War Comes to Josh, My Findings

Timeline (Left to right)

Sunday Feb 4, 1917 Reports of war with Germany	March 1917 U-boast sink 3 American merchant ships	April 2, 1917 President Wilson asks Congress for a declaration of war April 2, 1917 Joshua Henry Bates' 22nd birthday
June 5, 1917 Josh registers for the draft	July 3, 1917 Joshua helps with the draft registration in Park City, Utah	July 26, 1917 Josh picks up proofs of his studio photo
July 27, 1917 Josh visits family and friends, SLC, Springville, Spanish Fork	August 7, 1917 Joshua is called for his military service physical examination in Park City, Utah	August 16, 1917 Josh takes the teachers examination all day
August 17, 1917 More teacher examinations in the forenoon	August 17, 1917 1:00 PM Josh's physical examination	August 17 & 18, 1917 Visits with Everett and visits Selbys to hear their player piano
August 23, 1917 Josh attends a farewell party for Roy Haner who enlisted in the Marine Corps.	September 11, 1917 2nd day of school in Echo, new position	September 15. 1917 At 8:00 AM Josh goes to the Post Office and receives the call to duty the next Wednesday. He works on the car, goes to dinner, picks up his clothes and books from Echo and goes back to Coalville for the night.
September 16, 1917 Josh skipped church. He and Parley go to Roy, Utah to see Vera, then Uncle Tom.	September 17, 1917 Josh stopped for fruit and goes to Rena Smith's house. They go to a farewell party at night. Bert and Josh speak.	September 18, 1917 Josh writes letters, then goes to the Smiths at night.
September 19, 1917 Josh reports for military service. His parents take it hard.	September 20, 1917 Josh and others leave Utah for Camp Lewis.	

Photograph: Josh paid for a photograph now as he knew the French, Germans, British and other young soldiers have died in the millions. He had better have a current photographic memory of himself. A less bleak purpose is professional use or as a gift for Rena.

Journal from September 11-17, 1917: I can really tell his penmanship on Saturday September 15th was different. His handwriting was slanting in different directions and it looked like he was pressing hard with the pen here and there and the pen was running out of ink without him refilling it. No wonder, he received his call to duty. Statistically he knew that there was a chance he would serve, but I am sure he hoped to teach and to get married instead.

Transcription of Page 101 of his journal, September 18-19, 1917:

a good time. Bert & I make a little speech. Home 1:30 A.M.

Tue. Sept 18 Work in field some to-day write letters. Home in early part of evening Over to Smiths at night Home 1:20

Wed. Sept 19 To day I leave to put myself under military service. I shall no doubt find myself in a new experience The folks take my leaving quite hard. It makes it harder for me but I must bare up. Will try and continue my journal. We l leave Utah Tomorrow.

A Farewell to Soldier Boys Article

1. The ball was given as Mr. Nichols and Miss Thompson felt that the draftees and volunteers leaving for The Great War were not given a good community sendoff. Rasband Hall and all entertainment and décor and food were donated.
2. The ticket proceeds were given to the soldiers honored at the ball.
3. The article is in the September 14, 1917 *Park Record.* (I found the date online).
4. They will leave next Thursday morning, September 20, 1917, for Camp Lewis.
5. Joshua had not received his call to duty until the morning after this article was published. He took Rena to the ball. He mentions that he and Bert both made speeches at the event.

Good-Bye, God Speed, Safe Return! Article points:

1. Lots of apathy about their departure, but the truly loyal came to say goodbye.
2. There was an early-morning reverie and some members of the Park City Military Band playing.
3. Some were tearful, some jolly of the hundreds who assembled at 6:30 AM.
4. The boys traveled in Pullman tourists and will travel directly to Camp Lewis.
5. Names of those in the "second call" were republished, including Joshua.
6. The ball was reviewed, mentioning that each boy received an American flag pin and proceeds from their tickets, $4.00 each for a tobacco fund.
7. Three men enlisted.
8. Prose of the time: "the flower of American manhood is becoming involved in this great world's struggle…"

Transcription:

Joshua H Bates
Co D #347 M.G. Bn.
Identification number
2,225,462
Two million, two hundred and fifty-five thousand, four hundred and sixty two.

Chapter 16: Camp Lewis, Washington, My Findings

Transcription of Page 1 of little diary:
Journal of J.H. Bates
Wanship, Utah.

Sept. 19 1917 Wed.
Report at Sheriffs office for military service We are told that we must be ready to take the train at Park City at 6:00A.M. Back to Wanship. To party at night. Presents given me were pen from Parley Watch from father & mother and a ring from the people of the town

Thurs. Sept 20, 1917
Up all night. Leave for Park City with Bert, Edd and Sid at 4:30. Breakfast and take train

Answers:
Page 2:

Towns train went through were Park City, Wanship, Coalville, Echo, Ogden. His mother, Mrs. Smith, Mrs. Homer, Stella and Rena came to Echo. The next state they entered was Idaho.

Page 3:

Portland is in Oregon. Once at Camp Lewis the draftees visited the doctors, given their quarters, went to dinner, and listened to a lecture. Josh complains about the damp, cold weather.

Letters Home Answers:
Oct 1, 1917 :

"Shanks Ponies" are soldiers that walk on their own, without horses. There are only 4 horses in the company but 172 men. Four companies make up the 346th M.G. Bn, which is his abbreviation for "Machine Gun Battalion."

Oct 12, 1917:

Drills are getting more complex and longer, but are interesting. Josh has had no trouble keeping up.
He likes watching the "greenies", but muses that a few weeks ago he was in their place.
He attends a school each night from 6:30-8:00 PM.
Time off comes on Wednesday afternoons, Saturday afternoons and Sunday. Those are the days when he writes. Otherwise they drill 8 hours a day.

December 29, 1917 Postcard Home:

The camp is quarantined due to scarlet fever. The writer says that "Joshie," Ed and Bert are doing fine. Anne Young wrote the card for them.

Diary

Sunday Nov 4

Josh was on stable detail and wrote in the afternoon. He mentioned that there was a football game in the morning and their team won. He received a letter from Rena.

Monday

His pay was $42.

He was detailed to do clerical work at the base hospital.

He received letters from his mother and Lila Bates, and candy from Rena.

Tuesday, Dec 25.

The barracks was under quarantine so his father, who planned on visiting, could not come. Josh spent the day reading and writing letters. They had a "big feed" at supper. Josh mentioned that it was the first Christmas away from home. He wondered if people missed him as much as he missed them. Then he adds that he was glad to be missed. Another barracks paraded by their barracks in the evening.

The Telegram

1. The original of the telegram was Camp Lewis Washington.
2. The date was Jan 29, 1918.
3. The recipient was Joshua Bates Sr.
4. The telegram was delivered to the Park Hotel in Tacoma, Washington.
5. The sender was Joshua
6. The time of the telegram was 12:42 PM.
7. It was a Western Union Telegram and the office in Tacoma is always open.
8. The proof that the meeting happened was the photograph of Joshua Henry and his father together. His father also took a photograph of Joshua working at a pup tent. The postcard mentions that Father arrived and was enjoying himself.

Bonds and Insurance and Recommendations

1. Josh is paying for bonds by an automatic withdrawal from his paycheck. He wonders if he should save more.

2. The value of his $10,000 life insurance policy would be worth $172,645.98 Annual Inflation: 2.95% Total Inflation: 1626.46% (http://www.dollartimes.com/inflation/inflation.php?amount=10000&year=1918).

3. Characteristics: Man of ability and promise, dependable, clean, unaddicted, good habits, wholesome character, good record as a teacher.

The Weather/Journal

The weather in Utah is usually sunny and hot, or cold and clear. The Northwest rain and humidity was a new experience for him, and since he mentioned it often, even from the first day at Camp Lewis, I conclude that he did not care for it at all.

March 1918/Journal

He was sick and in bed for an extended period of time. He was even a patient in the hospital. When he went back to the barracks he still needed to rest.

May 12, 1918 Letter Home

It is Mother's Day and he wished that he were home to spend it with his mother.
He realized how good his mother was to him.
In fact, he wondered if others have as good a parents as he did.
He said their guidance was the best any parents could give.
Their training is serving him well now.
He wanted to be worthy of the trust given to him.

I would cry if I received such a letter from a child. He must have been a very grateful and good person. I am thankful that my parents cared for me and taught me many skills and beliefs that I have used all my life.

Chapter 17: Off to France, My Findings

Last letter from the United States:

Its date was July 4, 1918 and he was in New York City. He felt he needed at least two weeks there with lots of money to spend.

Company D Photograph:

There is no way they were in France March 1918. Most of them were terribly sick in the Camp Lewis Hospital. My theory is that the official photographs were taken at Camp Lewis and that they later were stationed "near Chateau de Lonne." Why would anyone claim this?

The Ulysses:

The Red Cross postcard did not say where the ship landed. I imagine it was for the soldiers' safety.

The Letter to Parley:

The letter has a notation of "O.K. Arthur E. Carlson 2nd D_ chef R.C." On the envelop he signed again below "Censored" and there is also a "Passed as Censored" eagle stamp. I don't see any words crossed out in this letter about farming, so Josh did a fine job not giving any secrets away from "Somewhere in France."

Chapter 18: The Meuse-Argonne Offensive, My Findings

The 347th:

1. The A.E.F. advance on Gesnes was the most intense action for the 181st Brigade, in which the 347th M.G.Bn fought.
2. The Brigade held their conquered position from September 30th to October 3rd.
3. Company D was at the center of the held line.
4. The enemy was constantly pelting them with shell-fire
5. The 32rd came on October 3, 1917 to relieve the division, but the 181st did not get to rest like the other brigade.
6. The Brigade was reassigned and headed up to the front line.
7. The 347th MG Bn was relieved on October 3, 1917.

Relief of the 91st Division Order:

1. Major General George H Cameron wrote the order.
2. It was addressed to the Commanding General of the 91st Division.
3. The subject was the relief of the 91st Division
4. The 91st was to be relieved from the front line tonight (Oct 3, 1918) and placed in Corps Reserve.

5. They had done their full share in the forward push of the Army being entitled to reorganize and rest.
6. The Division was established as a reliable fighting unit, with splendid behavior and a brilliant record, pushing ahead and clinging to every yard gained.
7. George H. Cameron signed the order.

What does this have to do with Josh?

Josh was killed the day after the order. He was very cheerful about Company D and all the 91st Division being relieved. Actually, most had marched out the night before with the arrival of the 32rd Division. He had taken a message to an isolated Company D platoon about the relief. On his return to a dugout to report, a pair of "bracket shell" fragments struck him high in the chest and he died instantly. It was reported that all he said was, "Oh." He was killed in the southeast corner of the Bois de Baulney, about a half mile from the Bois de Cierges. He was buried where he died. The soldier next to him, Sergeant Frank Bedell, was not hurt. His captain since Camp Lewis, Captain Thomas, said that Josh was "exceptionally conscientious…a cheerful soldier…a high class man." He was the last man killed before the 347th was relieved on this date.

How heart-breaking for his parents to receive back letters to him with "Killed Oct 4 18" scrawled on them and with stamps reading "DECEASED verified by STATISTICAL DIVISION H.A.E.F."

The Telegram:

1. Date sent: Nov 6, 1918
2. From: Harris. The Adjutant General
3. To: Mr. Joshawa Bates (spelling on telegram)
4. Joshuah Bates (spelling on telegram)
5. Date of death: October 4, 1918
6. Origin: Washington D. C.
7. Delivered to: Wanship Summit County Utah

Captain Thomas' Description of Josh:

1. High regard as a soldier and a gentleman
2. He upheld the best traditions of the American Army in France.
3. Cheerfulness and willingness to do his duty in trying circumstances
4. A severe loss to the company (Josh served them all is what I interpret from this)

Captain Thomas knew Josh since he arrived at Camp Lewis, training him and then working with him in France. He was an excellent first-hand witness to Josh's character.

I am amazed that the Google Earth area and forests are shaped exactly the same as the drawing in 1918. I would have thought those forests would have been destroyed. You can see clearly that the death report was exact in mentioning his grave site. Knowing that the two forests were only about a half mile from tip to tip helps with knowing the lay of the land.

Lieutenant Price's Letter:

1. Price last saw Josh on September 29, 1918, just before the lieutenant was wounded.
2. He had known Josh since Camp Lewis, September 21, 1918.
3. Honest, loyal, upright, faithful, courageous, disciplined, invaluable carrying messages for the company, someone to be proud of as a man, as a son, and as a soldier.
4. Price was one of his officers.
5. Price took Josh with him as a messenger when they passed through a "great deal" of enemy fire.
6. Josh was working at company headquarters the day Price was wounded.
7. Lieutenant H. W. Price, 347th Machine Gun Battalion, AEF
8. Since Price had been in the hospital since September 29, 1918 his information was incomplete regarding Josh's death. In fact, he is hoping that the death report was in error. However, he did add more detail about Josh's duties.

The American Red Cross Letter:

1. The American Red Cross
2. They took photographs of the dead soldiers' graves to send to family or emergency contact persons. They mentioned that they did their best to take accurate photographs of locations, but noted that often the remains were moved on to better locations to care for the bodies.
3. Three photographs were provided.
4. The letter inferred that the photographs were on the way, if I interpret the tense of "are being sent" correctly.
5. The photograph could not have been at the Bois de Baulney. Josh's body was moved!

Chapter 19: Coming Home, My Findings

Errors in Josh's Obituary:

1. He was not operating a machine gun at the time of death.

2. High School is not capitalized, being part of a location name.

Telegram Proof:
The telegraph from Hoboken, New Jersey states that Joshua **P** Bates will be leaving Jersey City at midnight September 3, 19__ being transported to Wanship, Utah via Union Pacific Railroad.

Double Exposure:

When everyone used film that needed developing, the film had to advance through the camera body to capture each photograph. The photographer had to remember to turn a button or crank to advance the film to the next section ready for the next photograph. If he or she forgot, the next photograph would interpose on the previous one. In this photograph the caisson carrying Josh's body was overlaid with a photograph of a close-up of his flag-draped coffin. I wonder if the young man to the right was his younger brother Roy?

Headstone Transcription:

1. Joshua H. Bates
2. April 2, 1895
3. Oct. 3, 1918 (most sources say Oct. 4, 1918)
4. Co D. 347 M.G. Bn.
5. Killed in France
6. Two crossed American flags
7. Evergreen tree…symbol of the 91st Division "Always Ready", also can be a symbol of eternal life
8. Laurel sprigs
9. American Legion bronze marker

Additional Information from Joshua's War Service Questionnaire:

1. His commanding officer was major J.C. McCanstland
2. Joshua was at Camp Lewis for 9 months.
3. He attended school in France.
4. Josh was made a 1st Class Private on December 1, 1917.
5. He was engaged at St Mihiel, Meuse-Argonne.
6. He was cited for gallantry on January 2, 1919.

7. He was transported over sees on July 5, 1918.
8. He was an active member of the LDS Church.
9. He was killed in action on October 3, 1918. (All other sources but his headstone say October 4, 1918).
10. He was killed while delivering a message of relief to an isolated platoon. (The official report indicated that he died when he returned).

Statistics of the 347th

Killed: 37

Mortality of the 91st Division

896

91st Division Name and Design

Name: Wild West Division

Design: Green fir tree

Symbolism: Readiness and usefulness

Source Notes

The following notes refer to the sources in each chapter. Each brief citation includes information to identify the references cited from the Selected Bibliography. All original materials are shared in each chapter, through either a digital copy or a digital photograph.

i. COVER

a. Joshua Henry Bates collage by Joan Enders, 1898-1917, Bates Family Collection.

ii. PREFACE

a. Chandler, M. "Study: Teen's knowledge of family history a sign of social-emotional health." February 28 2014.

b. Duke, M., & Fivush, R. "Knowledge of family history as a clinically useful index of psychological well-being and prognosis: A brief report," 268-272.

c. Wineberg, S. "Thinking Like a Historian." 1 January 2011.

1. THE SUSPECT

a. Joshua Henry Bates. Photograph, July 1917, Bates Family Collection.

b. "1910s in Western Fashion."

c. "A Guide to Men's Dress Shirt Collars."

2. STARTING AT THE END

a. "Summit County Boy Dies for World Liberty," Bates Family Collection.

3. EVERYONE HAS A FAMIY: THE U.S. CENSUS

a. 1900 U.S. Census, Wanship Precincts, Utah, pop. Sch., ED 138, p. 118-A, Joshua H. Bates; FamiySearch.org.

b. 1910 U.S. Census, Wanship Precinct, Utah, pop. Sch., ED 69, p. 2-B, Joshua H. Bates; FamilySearch.org.

4. READING FAMILY DATA CHARTS

a. A Parley Bates. Joshua Bates-Eliza Petersen Family Group Sheet, Bates Family Group Sheet 1869-1958; supplied by Margaret Enders, Longview, Washington, 2009.

5. EVERYONE HAS A FAMILY: PHOTOGRAPHS

a. Joshua and Eliza Petersen family photograph, ca. summer 1917, Bates Family Collection.

b. Three Eldest Bates Children photograph, ca. February 1906, Bates Family Collection.

c. Joshua Bates Toddler photograph, ca. 1898, Bates Family Collection.

d. "Boys' Hair Styles." *Historical Boy Clothing.*

6. WHAT PHOTOGRAPHS REVEAL

a. Four Bates children photograph, ca. 1917, Bates Family Collection.

7. RECORDS OF JOSH'S YOUTH

a. "A Splendid Audience Greeted the Eighth Grade Graduates Monday Evening Last," Bates Family Collection.

b. School Registration, 1911-1014; Summit Stake Academy, Bates Family Collection.

c. Church of Jesus Christ of Latter-day Saints, (Wanship, Summit, Utah) Ordinance Summary, 1895-1912 (privately held by J. Lambert Bates, North Ogden, Utah, 2011).

d. Wanship School Student photograph, ca. 1907-8, privately held by J. Lambert Bates, North Ogden, Utah, 2011).

e. "Commencement Exercises of the Class of 1915 North Summit High School," May 1915' Summit Stake Tabernacle, Coalville, Utah, Bates Family Collection.

8. UNIVERSITY DAYS

a. "University of Utah, Aerial," ca. 1920, digital image, University of Utah.

b. School registration and receipts, 1915-1916, University of Utah, Bates Family Collection.

c. County teacher certificate, 1915, Bates Family Collection.

d. County teacher certificate, 1916, Bates Family Collection.

e. University of Utah receipt, 1916, Bates Family Collection.

9. JOSHUA'S JOURNAL BEGINS.

a. Bates, "Journal of Joshua H. Bates," p. 1., Bates Family Collection.

10. ON THE TOWN

a. Historic Salt Lake City photographs, ca. 1910-1920, digital images, *Utah History to Go.*

b. Bates, "Journal of Joshua H. Bates," pp. 13,15-16.

c. "Train ticket, ca 1916," Bates Family Collection.

11. SWEET ON SOMEONE

a. Bates, "Journal of Joshua H. Bates," PP. 15, 17, 20, 22-3, 25, 27, 47, 53-4, 58-61, 64, 72, 75, 77-8, 82, 87, 89-90, 97.

b. "JB" neck scarf, ca. 1917, Bates Family Collection.

c. Joshua H. Bates and Rena Smith, photograph, Bates Family Collection.

12. JOSH THE POET

a. Bates, "Mother," poem, ca. 1918. Bates Family Collection.

13. ALL IN A DAY'S WORK

a. Bates, "Journal of Joshua H. Bates," pp. 4-5, 7, 9-10, 30, 61, 99.

b. Wanship School, photograph ca. 1912, digital image, Summit County Utah.

c. Bates' desk, privately held by Phyllis Bates Brown, Taylorsville, Utah.

d. North Summit High School basketball team and coach, photograph, privately held by J. Lambert Bates, North Ogden, Utah.

e. Echo Canyon School, photograph, ca. 1914, digital image, Summit County Utah.

14. JOSH ON JOSH

a. Bates, "Journal of Joshua H. Bates," pp. 3, 25, 47, 62, 64, 69-70, 95.

15. WAR COMES TO JOSH

a. *The U.S. Army in World War I, 1917-1918*, 10 September 2015.

b. Bates, "Journal of Joshua H. Bates," pp. 54, 64, 80, 91, 95-6, 100-1.

c. *National Archives*, Selective Service System, Joshua Henry Bates (A 43-1-27).

d. "Summit County Draft List," 7 July 1917, Park City (Utah), *The Park Record*, p. 3, col 7.

e. *National Archives*, "Military Records: World War I Draft Registration Cards," http://www.archives.gov/research/military/ww1/draft-registration/utah.html.

f. FamilySearch.org, "United States World War I Draft Registration Cards, 1917-1918," https://familysearch.org/search/collection/1968530.

g. Bates Family Archives, Notice of call…., Letter, 1917, Bates Family Collection.

h. "A Farewell to Soldier Boys," Park City (Utah), *The Park Record*, 14 September 1917, p. 1.

i. i. "Good-Bye, God Speed, Safe Return!" Park City (Utah), *The Park Record*, 21 September 1917, p. 1.

j. "The Call to Duty Join the Army," digital poster, Library of Congress, http://www.loc.gov/pictures/item/00651808, accessed 27 April 2016.

16. CAMP LEWIS, WASHINGTON

a. Bates, "Journal of J. H. Bates, Camp Lewis, n.p.

b. Lewis-McChord Website, "Lewis Army Museum," digital image.

c. Joshua Henry Bates to "Father," 1 October 1917; 12 October 1917, J. Lambert Bates Collection.

d. "Mess line," Postcard, ca. 1917, Bates Family Collection.

e. "Training," Postcard, ca. 1917, Bates Family Collection.

f. "Barracks," Postcard, ca. 1917, Bates Family Collection.

g. "Park Hotel," Postcard, ca. 1917, Bates Family Collection.

h. Bates, Joshua Henry to "Dear Mother," January 1918.

i. Joshua to "Joshua Bates Sr," 29 January 1918, J. Lambert Bates Collection.

j. Joshua Henry Bates, photograph, January 1918, J. Lambert Bates Collection.

k. County Attorney to "To Whom It May Concern," 10 December 1917, J. Lambert Bates Collection.

l. Joshua Henry Bates to "Dear Mother and Father," 12 May 1918, J. Lambert Bates Collection.

m. "Bon Voyage Poster," digital poster, 91st Division Publication Committee.

17. OFF TO FRANCE

a. Joshua Henry Bates to "Family," 1 October 1917; 4 July 1918.

b. Calkins, "Company D, near Chateau De Lonne, Marcy 1918," [plate p. 120-1].

c. HMAT Ulysses, digital photograph, 1 March 1916, Australian War Memorial.

d. "Soldier's Mail," postcard, ca. July 1918.

e. "Souvenir de France," handkerchief, ca. July 1918.

f. Joshua H. Bates, to "A. Parley Bates," 16 August 1918, J. Lambert Bates Collection.

18. THE MEUSE-ARGONNE OFFENSIVE

a. Calkins, p. 24.

b. Calkins, McDonald photograph, p. 129.

c. Cameron, 3 October 1918.

d. Dyment, p. 17.

e. Mrs. Joshua Bates to "Mr. Joshua H. Bates", ca. August-October 1918.

f. "Roll of Honor: Joshua Bates, Wanship, Utah, Is reported killed in action on today's casualty list," Bates Family Collection.

g. Harris to "Mr. Joshawa Bates," 6 November 1918.

h. Edwin S. Thomas to "Mrs. Joshua Bates," 4 December 1918.

i. Grave Pvt Joshua Bates, map, 1918.

j. Bois Communal de Baulney, map.

k. H. W. Price to "My dear Mrs. Bates," 21 December 1918.

l. Calkins, n.p.

m. American Red Cross to "The Relatives of Our American Dead," 12 February 1919.

n. Joshua H. Bates, grave photograph, ca. 1918, Bates Family Collection.

o. Calkins, roster, p. 118.

p. Calkins, commendation, p. 31.

19. Coming Home

a. "Summit County Boy Dies for World Liberty," Bates Family Collection.

b. Remains Telegram J. Lambert Bates Collection.

c. Graves Registration Service to "Joshua Bates," 3 September ca. 1921.

d. Utah funeral photograph, ca. 1921, Bates Family Collection.

e. Headstone, photograph, 2012, Bates Family Collection.

f. World War I service questionnaire, series 85298, reel 2.

g. Military service cards, series 85268, reel 2.

h. Utah State Archives, veterans with federal service buried in Utah, FHL microfilm 485,498.

i. New River Notes Website, 91st Badge, digital image, April 2015.

j. Pershing, John J., "United States Army in Memory Of," certificate, n.d., J. Lambert Bates Collection.

k. Calkins, p. 38.

Bibliography

"1910s in Western Fashion." Wikipedia Commons. https://en.wikipedia.org/wiki/File:Manandhisdog1916.jpg, accessed 10 November 2015.

A. Parley Bates. Joshua Bates-Eliza Petersen Family Group Sheet, Bates Family Group Sheet 1869-1958, supplied by Margaret Enders, Longview, Washington, 2008.

Alseen Studios. classified ad. *Salt Lake Tribune*, 30 June 1913. Online archives. https://newspapers.lib.utah.edu : accessed 12 November 2015.

American Red Cross (Washington, D. C.) to "The Relatives of Our American Dead" [Wanship, Utah]. Form letter. 12 February 1919. Privately held by Margaret Enders, Longview, WA, 2010.

Bates Family Collection. Privately held by Margaret Enders, Longview, Washington, 2009.

Bates, Joshua H. (Camp Lewis, Washington) to "Family" [Wanship, Utah]. Letter. 4 July 1918. Privately held by J. Lambert Bates, North Ogden, Utah, 2012.

Bates, Joshua H. (somewhere in France) to "A Privately held by Margaret Enders, Longview, WA, 2010. Parley Bates" [Wanship, Utah]. Letter. 16 August 1918. Privately held by J. Lambert Bates, North Ogden, Utah, 2012.

Bates, Joshua H. Wood secretary desk. Furniture, ca. 1915. Privately held by Phyllis Bates Brown, Taylorsville, Utah.

Bates, Joshua Henry (Camp Lewis, Washington) to "Dear Mother and Father [Wanship, Utah]. Letter. 12 May 1918. Privately held by J. Lambert Bates, North Ogden, Utah, 2012.

Bates, Joshua Henry. (Camp Lewis, Washington) to "Father" [Wanship, Utah]. Letter. 1 October 1917. Privately held by J. Lambert Bates, North Ogden, Utah, 2013.

Bates, Joshua Henry. (Camp Lewis, Washington) to "The drill" [Wanship, Utah]. Letter. 12 October 1917. Privately held by J. Lambert Bates, North Ogden, Utah, 2013.

Bates, Joshua Henry. "Journal of J. H. Bates." Journal. Camp Lewis, Washington, 1917-1918. Private Privately held by Margaret Enders, Longview, WA, 2010.

Bates, Joshua Henry. "Journal of Joshua H. Bates [1916-1917]". Privately held by Margaret Enders, Longview, Washington, 2009.

Bates, Joshua Henry. Grave Photograph, ca. 1918. American Red Cross, Verdun, France. Privately held by Margaret Enders, Longview, WA, 2010.

Bates, Joshua Henry. Photographs, January 1918. Privately held by Margaret Enders, Longview, WA, 2010.

Bates. Joshua Henry. "Mother." Poem, ca. 1918. Privately held by Margaret Enders, Longview, Washington, 2009.

Bate, Joshua Henry (Somewhere in France) to "A. Parley Bates. Letter. 16 August 1918. Bates, Mrs. Joshua (Wanship, Utah) to "Mr. Joshua H. Bates" [France] ca. August-October 1918. Privately held by J. Lambert Bates, North Ogden, Utah, 2012.

Bates, Mrs. Joshua (Wanship, Utah) to "Mr. Joshua H. Bates" [France] ca. August-October 1918. Privately held by J. Lambert Bates, North Ogden, Utah, 2012.

Bois Communal de Baulney," Digital map. Google Earth, http://googleearth.com. October 2007.

Bon Voyage Poster." *The Story of the 91st Division.* San Francisco, CA: 91st Division Publication Committee, 1919.

"Boys' Hair Styles." *Historical Boy Clothing* (http://histclo.com/style/head/hair/hairbs.html : accessed 17 April 2015.

Cabinet Card. http://genealogy.about.com/od/photo_dating/p/cabinet_card.htm : 17 April 2016.

Calkins, J. Uberto. *History of the 347th Battalion: Compiled from Official Records and the Personal Notes of Various Members of the Battalion.* Oakland, CA: Horwinsk, 1919.

The Call to Duty Join the Army." Digital poster, [n.d.]. Library of Congress. http://www.loc.gov/pictires/item/00651808. Accessed 27 April 2016.

Cameron, George C. "Relief of 91st Division. Digital text. *Headquarters Fifth Army Corps, 3 October 1918. 91st Division, American Expeditionary Force, World War I.* http://www.newrivernotes.com/ww1/91divae.htm. 27 April 2015.

Camp Lewis/Tacoma. Postcards, ca. 1917-1918. Privately held by Margaret Enders, Longview, WA, 2010.

Chandler, M. "Study: Teen's knowledge of family history a sign of social-emotional health." *Washington Post.* http://www.washingtonpost.com/local/education/study-teens-knowledge-of-family-history-a-sign-of-social-emotional-health/2013/12/10/72fb7606-61ce-11e3-bf45-61f69f54fc5f_story.html, February 28 2014.

Church of Jesus Christ of Latter Day Saints (Wanship, Summit, Utah), Ordinance Record Summary, 1895-1912. Privately held by J. Lambert Bates, North Ogden, Utah, 2011.

County Attorney (Coalville, Utah) to "To Whom It May Concern" [Camp Lewis, Washington]. Letter. 10 December 1917. Privately held by Margaret Enders, Longview, WA, 2010.

Duke, M., & Fivush, R. "Knowledge of family history as a clinically useful index of psychological well-being and prognosis: A brief report." *Psychotherapy Theory, Research, Practice, Training,* June 2008: 268-272.

Dyment, Colin V., Lt A.R.C., 91st Division. "347th Machine Gunn Battalion, 91st Division Casualty Report." American Red Cross. Seattle, WA 22 July ca. 1919.

Echo Canyon School. Photograph, ca. 1914. Digital image. Summit County, Utah, http://www.co.summit.ut.us.

FamilySearch.org, "United States World War I Draft Registration Cards, 1917-1918," https://familysearch.org/search/collection/1968530.

Graves Registration Service (unknown location) to "Joshua Bates." [Wanship, Utah]. Telegram. 3 September 19__. Privately held by Margaret Enders, Longview, WA, 2010.

"A Guide to Men's Dress Shirt Collars." Hugh & Crye. Washington, DC 20003. https://www.hughandcrye.com/pages/dress-shirt-collars : 2 November 1914.

Harris. The Adjutant General. (Washington D. C.) to "Mr. Joshawa Bates" [Wanship, Utah]. Telegram. 6 November 1918. Privately held by J. Lambert Bates, North Ogden, Utah, 2012.

Headstone of Joshua H. Bates. Digital photograph. July 2012. Privately held by Margaret Enders, Longview, WA, 2010.

Historical Salt Lake City Photographs, ca. 1910-1920. Digital. Utah History to Go, http://heritage.utah.gov, 2014.

HMAT Ulysses. Digital Photograph. Australian War Memorial. https://www.aw.gov.au/colletion/PB1095/. 27 April 2016.

Joshua. (Camp Lewis, Washington) to "Joshua Bates Sr" [Tacoma, WA]. Telegram. Privately held by J. Lambert Bates, North Ogden, Utah.

Joshua H. Bates and Rena Smith. Photograph, ca. 1917. Privately held by Margaret Enders, Longview, Washington, 2009

Lewis Army Museum. Digital images. Lewis-McChord Website, http://wwwlewis-mcchord.army.mil : 15 April 2015.

Map, Grave Pvt. Joshua Bates." Bois Communal de Baulney, France: Company D 347 MGBat, 1918.

New River Notes Website, 91st Badge, digital image, , http://www.newrivernotes.com/topical_books_1918_worldwar1_storyof_91st_division.htm, April 2015.

North Summit High School basketball team and coach. Photograph, ca. 1916-1917. Privately held by J. Lambert Bates, North Ogden, Utah.

Pershing, John J., "United States Army in Memory," certificate, n.d., Privately held by J. Lambert Bates, North Ogden, Utah.

Price, H. W., Lieutenant. (Mesnes, France) to "My Dear Mrs. Bates" [Wanship, Utah]. Letter. 21 December 1918. Privately held by Margaret Enders, Longview, WA, 2010.

School Registrations and Receipts 1915-6. University of Utah. Privately held by Margaret Enders, Longview, Washington, 2009.

Soldiers' Mail." Postcard, ca. July 1918. American Red Cross. Privately held by Margaret Enders, Longview, WA, 2010.

Souvenir de France' Handkerchief." Ca. July 1918. Privately held by J. Lambert Bates, North Ogden, Utah, 2012.

A Splendid Audience Greeted the Eighth Grade Graduates Monday Evening Last." Utah. Park City. *Park Record*, 3 June 1911, p. 1.

Stake Academy, Coalville, Summit County, Utah. School Registration, 1911-1912. Privately held by Margaret Enders, Longview, Washington, 2009.

State of Utah, County Teacher Certificates. 1915-6. Privately held by Margaret Enders, Longview, Washington, 2009.

Summit County Boy Dies for World Liberty." Utah. Park City. *Park Record*, ca. November 1918. Privately held by Margaret Enders, Longview, Washington ,2009.

"Summit County Draft List." Utah. Park City. *Park Record*, 7 July 1917.

The U.S. Army in World War I, 1917-1918, http://history.army.mil/bppks/amb-v2/PDF/chapter01.pdf.

Thomas, Edwin. S., Captain. (France) to "Mr. Joshua Bates" [Wanship, Utah]. Letter. 4 December 1918. Privately held by Margaret Enders, Longview, WA, 2010.

"Train ticket, ca 1916." Ticket. Utah Light & Traction Company. Privately held by Margaret J. Enders, Longview, Washington. 2009.

United States, Selective Service System. *World War I Selective Service System Draft Registration Cards Index*, 1917-1918. Washington, D. C. : National Archives, database, http://www.archives.gov/research/military/ww1/draft-registration/utah.html.

University of Utah, Aerial." ca. 1920. Digital image. University of Utah. PediaView, http://pediaviewcom, Open Source Encyclopedia: accessed 2014.

Utah Education Association. Dues receipt, 1916. Privately held by Margaret Enders, Longview, Washington, 2009.

Utah Funeral. Double exposure photograph. Ca 1921. Privately held by Margaret Enders, Longview, WA, 2010.

Utah. Park City. *Park Record.* 14 September 1917.

Utah. Park City. *Park Record.* 21September 1917.

Utah State Archives and Records Service; Salt Lake City, Utah; *World War I Service Questionnaires, 1914-1918*; Creating Agency: *State Historical Society*; Series: *85298*; Reel: *2*.

Utah, Veterans with Federal Service Buried in Utah, Territorial to 1966," database with images, FamilySearch (https://familysearch.org/pal:/MM9.1.1/FLRQ-7J7: 6 December 2014), Joshua H Bates, 04 Oct 1918; citing City Cemetery, France, military unit Co D 347 MG Bn 91 Div, Army, World War 1, State Archives, Capitol Building, Salt Lake City; FHL microfilm 485,498.

Utah. Salt Lake City. *Salt Lake Telegram*. 13 November 1918. Web edition, http://www.newsbank.com. 27 April 2015.

Utah. Unknown city. Unknown newspaper. 20 November 1918.

Utah. Wanship Precincts, 1910 U.S. Census, population schedule. Database. The Church of Jesus Christ of Latter Day Saints. FamilySearch.org: accessed September 2009.

Utah. Wanship Precincts. 1900 U.S. Census, population schedule. Database. The Church of Jesus Christ of Latter Day Saints. FamilySearch.org: accessed September 2008.

Wanship School Students. Photograph. ca. 1907-8. Privately held by J. Lambert Bates, North Ogden, Utah, 2011.

Wanship School. Photograph, ca 1912. Digital image. Summit County, Utah, http://www.co.summit.ut.us.

Wineberg, S. "Thinking Like a Historian." *Library of Congress*. http://www.lc.gov/teachers.tps/quarterly/historical_thinking/article.html. 1 January 2011.

Acknowledgements

Many persons and educational needs came together to inspire the creation of a powerful inquiry learning experience, multiple conference and community presentations, a professional article, and finally, this book.

Talking with teachers and librarians, I realize that the same synchronicity involving these primary and secondary sources for the creations of this experience could be an insurmountable task for them. So thanks to their needs which propelled me into compiling this book and adding much, much more than they might need for the same inquiry learning.

My thanks to J. Lambert Bates who shared a wealth of materials with me. The journal and the letters were as a tasty ganache on my materials about Joshua. To the Washington State Library, my thanks for the "Social Studies CBA Grant" with which I facilitated learning experiences for my high school's social studies department. Thanks to the heavens for the epiphany that the primary sources about my uncle could be the basis of an inquiry experience for students about World War I and a soldier serving in France. A shout out to my partner in crime, J. D. Ott, who asked if we could replicate the inquiry lesson for his Advanced Placement students, then all his students, then the entire department's students. Grateful thanks to J.D. and Jodeana Kruse, my book cheerleaders.

My thanks to fellow writers of Writers Haven who gave encouragement and honest critiques of snippets of the book. My thanks to the participants of the American Night Writers Association Northwest Retreat who cleared my vision, and tutored me in the ways of publication. I am so grateful to Charlotte Lindstrom who read and questioned and improved my manuscript.

Lastly, to my husband, who witnessed joy, despair, anger, frustration, procrastination, celebration and whining as I pieced together a logical presentation that would be helpful to readers and instructors, for realizing that laundry and dinner extravaganzas would be on the back burner for a long, long time. I love you JerBear, and appreciate the space and understanding you gave me during the arduous labor and delivery of this printed child.

About the Author

Joan Enders served as a middle school and high school librarian. She was the recipient of the American Library Association's "Frances Henne Award" and has presented at dozens of library, social studies, language arts, community and genealogical societies and conferences. She has published many articles on research and librarianship in professional journals.

This is her first book, growing from a successful inquiry learning lesson in American history classes and a culmination of six year of case study research and testing. She is also a Follett School Solutions webinar trainer for librarians and has devoted years of service to her church.

Joan spends a gigantic chunk of time on genealogy but tweaks out more for quilting and visiting grandchildren and beach escapes. She and husband, Jerry, are cruising fans and looking forward to their next adventure. They are

Praise for the inquiry experience of...

Evidence is Lacking. Yet Still I Hope.

A Primary Source Glimpse into the Life of a World War I Soldier's Life...Home to Camp Lewis to France

"In over 20 years of teaching history, this story and activity were by far the best student interactive and engaged lesson I've taught. Students were drawn into Joshua's life, and wanted to know more when it was over, with one student wanting to contact Fort Lewis to see if they had more information about him.. Another student said, 'I wanted to cry when I found out what happened to him.' "

JD Ott APUSH Teacher

"The Joshua Bates experience provided one of the most lively, analytical and inquisitive discussions for my students all year. Older students still return and talk about their experience with his life story.

From a teacher's prospective, it allowed me to teach a skill set with a story rather than the other way around. The way his story is designed allows students to use skills I taught all year long and apply them like a historian or an investigator would. It was rewarding to finally see students put the puzzle together and present their findings."

Erin Flinn, American History Teacher

"Joan Enders worked tirelessly to research, archive and develop the story of Joshua Bates, sharing his life with countless students over the years. The end result of that work reside here, in this well-researched and written account of an ordinary man who was caught up in the extraordinary human tragedy of World War I. By telling the story of Joshua Bates, Joan gives voice to one of the thousands of American families who sacrificed so much to what was to have been 'the war to end all wars.' "

Paul Field, Historian and Teacher

High quality primary source kits of 40 of the most popular sources for a student inquiry experience are available directly from Alpine Books, 25 Alpine Way, Longview, Washington, 98632. The items are in color in order to show document aging, as well as truly colored items. Kits contain 8 x 11-inch materials, ready for lamination.

Custom primary source kits are available upon request, $2 per item up to 50 items.

Workshops for teachers, on–site or via webinar, are available; as are on-site or remote classroom debriefings for students.

Speaker or conference requests may be sent to Alpine Books, 25 Alpine Way, Longview, Washington 98632.

Educational Bonuses for multiple book purchases of *Evidence is Lacking. Yet I Still Hope.* are:

1. *The Essential Teacher's Guide for Evidence is Lacking. Yet I Still Hope.*, free with the purchase of ten (10) or more copies.
2. *Standard Primary Source Kit* (40 of the items I used during the inquiry lesson, high quality colored copies), free with the purchase of 20 or more books.
3. One classroom debriefing webinar with the author (30 minutes), free with the purchase of 30 or more copies.
4. Proof of purchase is required.

Complete pricing of supplemental materials are listed in the teacher guide and @ JoanEnders.com.

www.ingramcontent.com/pod-product-compliance
Lightning Source LLC
Chambersburg PA
CBHW080529090426
42733CB00015B/2528

* 9 7 8 0 9 9 9 0 1 4 4 0 0 *